"Spiritual disciplines, if done wrong, can become a form of sanctified narcissism. Bennett's book is a welcome corrective. He turns the disciplines sideways, and in doing so life gets oriented outward. We have focused much on the first great commandment. Bennett helps us put shoes on the second great commandment. After he discusses each spiritual discipline he gets down and dirty with specifics. If you take him seriously, your life and your neighborhood will be changed."

—**Dennis Okholm**, Azusa Pacific University;
author of *Dangerous Passions, Deadly Sins: Learning
from the Psychology of Ancient Monks*

"What if spiritual disciplines are not just for Sundays? And what if they are not just for your own spiritual growth? In this lively book, Kyle David Bennett shows how our everyday working and resting, speaking and listening, eating and shopping can be Christian practices *with* and *for* our neighbors. With earnest passion and humble humor, Bennett calls us to spiritual formation that is an intentionally social expression of love."

—**Rebecca Konyndyk DeYoung**, Calvin College;
author of *Glittering Vices*

D1113533

PRACTICES OF LOVE

✦ ✦ ✦ ✦ ✦ ✦ ✦ ✦ ✦ ✦ ✦ ✦ ✦ ✦ ✦

SPIRITUAL DISCIPLINES
FOR THE
LIFE OF THE WORLD

✦ ✦ ✦ ✦ ✦ ✦ ✦ ✦ ✦ ✦ ✦ ✦ ✦ ✦

KYLE DAVID BENNETT

Brazos Press

a division of Baker Publishing Group
Grand Rapids, Michigan

© 2017 by Kyle David Bennett

Published by Brazos Press
a division of Baker Publishing Group
PO Box 6287, Grand Rapids, MI 49516-6287
www.brazospress.com

Printed in the United States of America

All rights reserved. No part of this publication may be reproduced, stored in a retrieval system, or transmitted in any form or by any means—for example, electronic, photocopy, recording—without the prior written permission of the publisher. The only exception is brief quotations in printed reviews.

Library of Congress Cataloging-in-Publication Data
Names: Bennett, Kyle David, 1981– author.
Title: Practices of love : spiritual disciplines for the life of the world / Kyle David
    Bennett.
Description: Grand Rapids, MI : Brazos Press, a division of Baker Publishing Group,
    [2017] | Includes bibliographical references and index.
Identifiers: LCCN 2017013417 | ISBN 9781587434037 (pbk.)
Subjects: LCSH: Spiritual life—Christianity. | Christian life.
Classification: LCC BV4501.3 .B45765 2017 | DDC 248.4/6—dc23
LC record available at https://lccn.loc.gov/2017013417

Scripture quotations are from the New Revised Standard Version of the Bible, copyright © 1989, by the Division of Christian Education of the National Council of the Churches of Christ in the United States of America. Used by permission. All rights reserved.

17 18 19 20 21 22 23   7 6 5 4 3 2 1

In keeping with biblical principles of creation stewardship, Baker Publishing Group advocates the responsible use of our natural resources. As a member of the Green Press Initiative, our company uses recycled paper when possible. The text paper of this book is composed in part of post-consumer waste.

To Andrea—
*because **you** saved **my** life once,*
and continually.

✦ ✦ ✦ ✦ ✦ ✦ ✦ ✦ ✦ ✦ ✦ ✦ ✦ ✦ ✦ ✦ ✦ ✦ ✦ ✦

You shall love your neighbor as yourself.

—Jesus of Nazareth (Mark 12:31)

Come, let us go up to the mountain of the LORD,
to the house of the God of Jacob;
that he may teach us his ways
and that we may walk in his paths.

—Isaiah the prophet (Isa. 2:3)

The chief thing is to love others like yourself, that's the chief
thing, and that's everything; nothing else is wanted—you will
find out at once how to arrange it all. And yet it's an old truth
which has been told and retold a billion times—but it has not
formed part of our lives!

—Fyodor Dostoevsky, *The Dream of a Ridiculous Man*

✦ ✦ ✦ ✦ ✦ ✦ ✦ ✦ ✦ ✦ ✦ ✦ ✦ ✦ ✦ ✦ ✦ ✦ ✦

✦ ✦ ✦ ✦ ✦ ✦ ✦ ✦ ✦ ✦ ✦ ✦ ✦ ✦ ✦ ✦ ✦ ✦ ✦ ✦

Love seeketh not Itself to please,
Nor for itself hath any care;
But for another gives its ease,
And builds a Heaven in Hell's despair.
So sung a little Clod of Clay,
Trodden with the cattle's feet;
But a Pebble of the brook,
Warbled out these metres meet
Love seeketh only self to please,
To bind another to Its delight,
Joys in another's loss of ease,
And builds a Hell in Heaven's despite.

—William Blake,
"The Clod and the Pebble"

When one has once fully entered the realm of Love, the world—
no matter how imperfect—becomes rich and beautiful, it consists solely of opportunities for Love.

—Søren Kierkegaard

✦ ✦ ✦ ✦ ✦ ✦ ✦ ✦ ✦ ✦ ✦ ✦ ✦ ✦ ✦ ✦ ✦ ✦ ✦ ✦

CONTENTS

Foreword by James K. A. Smith   xi

Preface   xiii

Introduction: Spiritual Heroin—How Not to Get Fixed   1

1. Spiritual Disciplines and the Way of Love   17

2. "What Do You Have That You Did Not Receive?"   39
   Simplicity and Renewed Owning

3. Directions for Ruling the Mind   59
   Meditation and Renewed Thinking

4. This Is My Tummy, Which I Will Curb for You   77
   Fasting and Feasting and Renewed Eating

5. Time-Out for Adults   95
   Solitude and Renewed Socializing

6. Controlling the Chatterbox   113
   Silence and Renewed Talking

7. How to Make Friends and Empower People   129
   Service and Renewed Working

8. Work Hard, Consecrate Hard   147
   Sabbath Keeping and Renewed Resting

9. Who's Afraid of Love?   167
   Everyday Discipline for the Life of the World

Acknowledgments   179

Notes   182

Further Reading   188

Index   190

FOREWORD

Imagine a unique tree—one that grows in the soil of church fathers such as John Cassian and Gregory the Great, with roots that trace back to "old vines" in Abraham Kuyper and Søren Kierkegaard, and branches grafted from Dallas Willard and Richard Mouw. The fruit of such a tree is this book: a vision for *how* to "do life in the Spirit."

If I could, I'd insert *Practices of Love* as volume 1.5 in my Cultural Liturgies trilogy. Giants such as Dallas Willard and Richard Foster showed us the significance of the spiritual disciplines for sanctification: Jesus invites us to follow him by *doing what he does*, not just thinking God's thoughts after him. In *Desiring the Kingdom* (and *You Are What You Love*), I tried to provide an "ecclesiological assist" to their spiritual disciplines project, arguing for the communal, gathered practices of worship as the hub for those other spiritual disciplines—that sacramental worship is the heart of discipleship. But in *Practices of Love*, Kyle Bennett expands the frame and shows us another part of the picture: all these disciplines are undertaken not just for our own relationship to God but also as a way to love our neighbor.

In other words, the spiritual disciplines are how we learn to obey the greatest commandments (Matt. 22:36–40): this is both how you learn to love God with all your heart, soul, and mind *and* how you learn to love your neighbor as yourself. Bennett calls this "flipping the spiritual disciplines on their side"—approaching them not merely as vertical channels for cultivating our relationship with God but as horizontal conduits that direct us into loving what God loves, including our neighbors and God's creation. Through the disciplines the Spirit invites us to unlearn the habits that lead us to ignore, dismiss, or just plain walk all over our neighbors in their need and vulnerability. The spiritual disciplines are a workshop for crooked, broken culture makers.

Every facet of our Monday to Saturday lives comes into view here. This book is invasive: it's going to push its way into your eating and your spending. It's going to take hold of your smartphone and your calendar. It will insert its argument into your family and your friendships. But that's because all of them matter to God. The spiritual disciplines—the "practices of love"—are how we learn to live out the Kuyperian conviction that there is not a single square inch of creation that isn't claimed by Jesus. But Bennett reminds us that the creation-claiming Jesus also gives us the gift of these practices to "occupy" creation in ways that are faithful, life giving, and attentive to our neighbors. This is why Bennett rightly describes his project as "a Christian philosophy of public affairs." But don't let that scare you off: Bennett's lively prose and passionate verve will make you forget every caricature of the tweedy, elbow-patched philosopher. This is feisty Christian thinking with wit and wisdom and both eyes fixed squarely on the nitty-gritty realities of the proverbial "real world." Above all, this book is a thoughtful invitation to life like the new creatures that we are.

James K. A. Smith

PREFACE

If you picked up this book because you are looking for a new, hip, or updated book on spiritual disciplines, then you might as well throw it in the fire pit because you will find this to be a book fit for burning. But if you are someone who cares deeply about following Jesus to the ends of the earth while caring for and enjoying the manifold affairs of God's creation, then this book is for you. And if, by any chance, you are like me and you are tired of the way that we Christians go about our witness to the world through deliberations and debates about ethical norms and political policies, and you want to figure out exactly what following Jesus looks like on the ground, then this book is most assuredly for you.

This book is about spiritual disciplines, but it's unlike other books on the topic. I do not tell you how to practice spiritual disciplines; I only suggest how frequently we should practice them. I do not provide a theology for practicing them; I only remind us of biblical principles to keep in mind as we do them. I do not try to justify our practice of them; I only make plain their significance. There are plenty of other books out there that can provide a history of their practice, a theology to support and motivate you to practice them, and a user's guide for practicing them. But what's missing from the literature is how these disciplines relate to everything else we do as Christians. What's missing is how these disciplines offer different ways of doing everything we do as human beings, how we can do them in ways that honor and witness to Christ and work toward the well-being of our neighbor. What is missing is how to understand *life* in the Spirit in accordance with our original calling from the Father as human beings and the commission given to us by the Son as his disciples.

What I offer in this book is simple: a framework. I try to synthesize, thematize, and cast these seemingly random and strange practices in a different light so that we can see how they are related and central to God's story of creation, redemption, and renewal and to our participation in it. In doing so, I hope to show that these seemingly strange and random practices relate to our original calling from the Father as human beings, his commandments to us as his people, Jesus's commandments and commissions to us as his disciples, and the Spirit's convicting us and creating us into our Savior and King's image. The way of Jesus is a holistic and integrated life—it covers all aspects of living. Our spirituality, which I will suggest consists of doing life in the Spirit, doesn't involve bringing something new *into* our life or culling something *out of* it but rather entails submitting to Jesus *in* our everyday life. The Spirit is already working in creation to make all things new, and this includes sanctifying our lives to make us new creations.

What I show in these pages is that every day we do basic human activities in selfish ways that negatively affect the life of our neighbor. We do them with only ourselves in mind. And this way of doing them hurts our neighbor, even if we don't see it. The harm may seem small or minor, but it is significant and tangible. Our neighbor's livelihood is certainly affected. Rather than being separate from our concrete lives and everyday affairs, spiritual disciplines actually correct the harmful ways we do these mundane activities, and through them God invites us to love our neighbor in the most basic and fundamental things we do. We have to discipline our most basic human impulses to make space for our neighbor and care for her. These practices discipline our selfish, harmful ways so that we can live and be guided by the Spirit in our everyday activities. It is through doing this that we can truly love our neighbor and bring life to her world.

The way of Jesus does not involve endless private, mystical experiences that tickle our fancy. Rather, it is the transformation of mundane activities that have vast public implications for our neighbor. Many of us are blind to the ways that we oppress, neglect, and ignore our neighbor in the little things that we do every day. We have "blind spots" in our practice of love. We have coherent, solid, and persuasive views on sexuality, abortion, immigration, and taxation, for example, but we're not entirely aware of or intentional about what we do during the week. At the end of the day (or more precisely, during the day), when we are done with our deliberations and debates and we put away abstract concepts and universal principles, what happens? What are we like? What do we do in our daily deeds? Are we loving our neighbor in our everyday procedures and cultural practices? In theory we claim to love our neighbor, but do we love her "on the ground"? What does this entail for us as stay-at-home parents, patrons, consumers, or voters?

Though in articulation this is a trade book, in substance it is a Christian philosophy of public affairs—a program for following the wise example of Christ in our interpersonal world. This is discipleship with a spine and a face. This is following Jesus in the flesh. What would it look like to image Christ? What does it mean to image God or cocreate with him, be a disciple of Jesus Christ and represent him, or be renewed and made holy in the Spirit? What I offer here includes some phenomenological analysis, theological commentary, historical appropriation, and pastoral admonition in the lines and between them. I'll let the philosophers, professors, pastors, and pundits study or smash them. Ultimately, I hope that this is a book for you—the homemaker, the barista, and the actuary. I am most interested in what this book *does* for you at home, in the pew, and in the marketplace. I hope it resonates with you. I hope you find hope in the struggle. I hope it bears the fruit of a few new ideas, instills new passions, or instructs appropriate reactions in the future.

Practices of Love is a play on Søren Kierkegaard's *Works of Love*—a book that pierces me with conviction every time I put my grubby hands on it. If you want to explore what it truly means to follow Christ, look no further than Kierkegaard. In *Works of Love*, Kierkegaard helps us see that love for our neighbor will take many forms and demands many things of us. He shows us how love for our neighbor works. But we are left to discern how we can and should love our neighbor in the itty-bitty, little things that we do. We see the demand, but we are left wondering how the demand concretely plays out in our lives. I hope *Practices of Love* fulfills such a need, even if it's only a start. I hope it helps us see the trees of loving our neighbor, not only the forest. Together through Christ may we truly love our neighbor as ourselves, whole selves, and may we find ourselves in Christ as we love our neighbor.

INTRODUCTION
SPIRITUAL HEROIN

HOW NOT TO GET FIXED

"Don't do it," I said. "Don't do the forty-day fast—that's my suggestion."

My friend had hit a "spiritual rut," as he put it, sagging his lower lip. He told me that he had "a buddy who just finished a forty-day fast," and "man, it sounds like I need something like that!" He then asked me if I had any suggestions. It was the quickest shift from somberness to cheer I'd ever seen. He was struggling with the rut but stirred by the possibility of overcoming it. He knew the problem and the solution, and I watched as the wheels turned in his head. His sagging lip started to resurrect as he thought about the potential experience.

He knew that I had practiced fasting, and he was looking for guidance. At first I thought that by "suggestions" he was looking for edifying devotional literature to read during the fast. You know, something to "pump him up" and get him through this difficult time. I would have been ready to fire off a few suggestions at the drop of a hat—anything by Augustine, Bonaventure, Thomas Boston, Samuel

Rutherford, Søren Kierkegaard, or Eugene Peterson. But it became quite clear to me early in our conversation that he had nothing of the sort in mind. He was far more interested in acquiring some tips and tricks for getting through the forty days of fasting than he was in being edified or challenged in his pursuit.

I waited for a moment while he finished ordering his food. (Today was his "Fat Tuesday"—the gorge before the purge—and he chose the burger chain Five Guys as his Last Supper.) Reluctance sat in his eyes while excitement leapt from every one of his words. I held my tongue for a short while. And then a little longer. He continued to share what he was going through and what he hoped to get from his fast. I tried my hardest to keep quiet—I had been there before. I knew the excitement. I understood the motivation. But I had to tell him that I had experienced the failure. I had to tell him what I went through. I was foaming at the lips with caution. Yet I couldn't stand back and do nothing. I had to be honest with him. Eventually I caved.

"Don't do it," I said. "Don't do the forty-day fast—that's my suggestion." He paused and looked up at me. "Wait . . . what?" A flimsy tomato slithered from his sesame seed bun onto his napkin. With earnestness he looked for a smile indicating jest—surely, surely I must be kidding. (He and I did like to kid a lot, but now was not one of those times.) With every inkling of energy I could muster, I refrained from any smile or slight twinkle of the eye. I didn't want to give the wrong impression. "Be stone cold and sincere, Kyle," I kept telling myself. All my energy was concentrated in my face, focused on maintaining this stoic look. "Don't do it," I said again.

The more I said it, the more I felt confident in saying it. The more I said it to him, the more I believed it myself. I was convincing myself. "Don't do the forty-day fast." I spent the next hour of this Last Supper trying to persuade him that he shouldn't go through with the fast. "We should talk about this further," I said. He, however, and fasted for whole weekends. Every morning I read and studied the Bible to inspire and encourage me. I meditated on the woes of Job and whispered them in my prayers. I fasted and imagined Sarai's feelings in her times of trouble. I wondered if I could have Nehemiah's courage in my situation. Occasionally I emerged from my self-inflicted cave to use the lavatory.

After several weeks, not much happened. I didn't hear anything. I didn't *feel any better*. These disciplines didn't seem to be working. The dullness and emptiness began to take their toll. The fasting and "solituding" for days became laborious and boring. The extended periods of repetition—ugh. "Is this really worth it?" "When are they going to kick in and start working?" "God, where are you?!" "Maybe I'm doing all this incorrectly." These were my thoughts. Eventually I became disillusioned. I continued to pray, but the eagerness to practice solitude and fasting had died a quick death. I eventually stopped doing these practices. Apparently their "success rate" that year was at an all-time low. Or maybe they just didn't work after all. Or maybe I wasn't doing them correctly. That must be it. Whatever the reason, their impotence coupled with the fact that they were inconvenient to do led me to just give up on them. I was confident that God could still be experienced in less laborious and invasive ways, even if I had to wait.

This experience in my sophomore year and my friend's story mentioned above have a common thread. In our lived practice of spiritual disciplines—specifically our motivation and attitude—my friend and I treated these disciplines like a drug that would afford us an emotional "fix." We treated them like divine opiates that would help us reach spiritual euphoria. They were like heroin to us. We did them to be stimulated. We did them to get high. We wanted to feel good. Both of us needed some kind of "rush." He fasted to get himself out of his spiritual rut, and I fasted, meditated, and "solituded" to get out of those slums of doubt and despair in that sophomoric semester. He needed stimulation and excitement, and I needed to feel securely close to God. Both of us needed some resolution to a spiritual "crisis" or an adverse circumstance in our life. We hoped to be stimulated, aroused, moved, changed, uplifted, and, hopefully, "set on fire" by picking up these ancient disciplines.

Perhaps you, too, have practiced them this way or still do. You are not alone. Many of us nowadays treat spiritual disciplines like heroin. We turn to them in times of trouble—when we are emotionally low or in a rut—and we use them to get a "spiritual high." We use them to get emotional shots of Jesus juice, if you will. We practice them because we want to feel stimulated, excited, or inspired afterward. When they don't "work" or give us the result we're looking for, we adapt. We go from soft practices to hard ones: from studying the Bible every morning to fasting for an entire day. Or we go from "solituding" for the weekend to scheduling a silent retreat for a week. When we don't get the high or spiritual euphoria that we seek or expect, or when the issue, situation, or emotional state that prompted us to practice a given discipline doesn't get resolved, we increase the dosage, so to speak. Instead of fasting for one day, we up the dosage to three days. Then forty days. We go from practicing solitude for a few hours on a Saturday afternoon to camping out in our closet for the weekend.

Then, when the issue, situation, or emotional state has been re-solved, we stop doing the discipline and return to our daily life, our day-to-day routines. We go back to what we were doing before. This is also true of our corporate practice of these disciplines. Whenever we practice fasting or silence in church, it is most often done for a time and a season. We fast because it's Lent. Once Lent passes, we stop fasting. Or we have a time of silence because we are in deep distress over a social issue that is currently before Congress. Once the social issue has been decided or the media hype wears down, we move on. We go back to our regularly scheduled lives. We don't fast, meditate, serve, or practice silence and solitude all year. Why would we? We only need to do these practices when something is wrong—particularly when we don't feel close to God or we don't feel that God is close to us. And if asked whether we *view* these disciplines as drugs that give us this "fix," we would unequivocally *say* no. Nevertheless, this is how we *treat* them. This is how we *use* them.

When we step back and look at the big picture, we can identify three tendencies in our lived practice of these disciplines that are founded in and fueled by our search for stimulation and "positive" emotions. Let's call them the "Three I's" of North American Christian practice of spiritual disciplines: individualism, intellectualism, and instrumentalism. We tend to practice spiritual disciplines as individuals and for ourselves as individuals. We practice them in isolation or somewhere we can't be seen. If we do end up doing them in a corporate setting, for example, in a congregational worship service or a youth lock-in, we treat them as individual alone time with God—we may be with others, but this is between us and God. The individual benefit that we tend to pursue through these disciplines is an intellectual good. By this I mean we are most interested in acquiring a wider understanding of Jesus's ways, a greater knowledge of his power and work, or a stronger faith in him. And we use these disciplines as instruments to help us get this. Then, when we have what we need or complete what we set out to do, we're done with them. They are only temporary practices for us.

Flipping Spiritual Disciplines on Their Side

Years ago, when I was reflecting on these past experiences with spiritual disciplines and how I was practicing them, and to a large extent how we tend to practice them in North American democratic society, I came across a passage in the book of Isaiah. It really made me think about how I practiced spiritual disciplines and to what end.

> Shout out, do not hold back!
>> Lift up your voice like a trumpet!
> Announce to my people their rebellion,
>> to the house of Jacob their sins.
> Yet day after day they seek me
>> and delight to know my ways,
> as if they were a nation that practiced righteousness
>> and did not forsake the ordinance of their God;
> they ask of me righteous judgments,
>> they delight to draw near to God.
> "Why do we fast, but you do not see?
>> Why humble ourselves, but you do not notice?"
> Look, you serve your own interest on your fast day,
>> and oppress all your workers.
> Look, you fast only to quarrel and to fight
>> and to strike with a wicked fist.
> Such fasting as you do today
>> will not make your voice heard on high.
> Is such the fast that I choose,
>> a day to humble oneself?
> Is it to bow down the head like a bulrush,
>> and to lie in sackcloth and ashes?
> Will you call this a fast,
>> a day acceptable to the Lord?
>
> Is not this the fast that I choose:
>> to loose the bonds of injustice,
>> to undo the thongs of the yoke,
> to let the oppressed go free,
>> and to break every yoke?

Is it not to share your bread with the hungry,
　　and bring the homeless poor into your house;
when you see the naked, to cover them,
　　and not to hide yourself from your own kin?
Then your light shall break forth like the dawn,
　　and your healing shall spring up quickly;
your vindicator shall go before you,
　　the glory of the LORD shall be your rear guard.
Then you shall call, and the LORD will answer;
　　you shall cry for help, and he will say, Here I am.

If you remove the yoke from among you,
　　the pointing of the finger, the speaking of evil,
if you offer your food to the hungry
　　and satisfy the needs of the afflicted,
then your light shall rise in the darkness
　　and your gloom be like the noonday.
The LORD will guide you continually,
　　and satisfy your needs in parched places,
　　and make your bones strong;
and you shall be like a watered garden,
　　like a spring of water,
　　whose waters never fail.
Your ancient ruins shall be rebuilt;
　　you shall raise up the foundations of many generations;
you shall be called the repairer of the breach,
　　the restorer of streets to live in.

(Isa. 58:1–12)

What's going on here? Well, essentially God is telling the Israelites that they've been selfish in their practice of what we nowadays call "spiritual disciplines." Now in a sense, they have been doing everything that they're supposed to be doing. They have been doing these practices; they have been disciplining their lives. But in another sense, they have done nothing right and everything wrong. It was this passage that got me wondering: What are spiritual disciplines, and why should we do them? Why do we do them? Why does God want us to do them? Are individual benefit and intellectual goods all there is to be gained from them? Can these things actually be gained from them? Can and should we practice them to feel better? Are they meant to bring us closer to God? Are they only about experiencing God and being intimate with him? Can they actually bring us closer to God?

Many of us have been taught that spiritual disciplines are means for fostering "spiritual growth" and helping us grow in our knowledge and faith in Jesus Christ.[6] We have been taught to see these practices as ways of experiencing our risen Lord and knowing him on a deeper level. We have practiced them to understand, know, and experience him. And maybe some good things have come from this. But like the ancient Israelites, maybe quite a few of us were oblivious to the fact that along the way, we oppressed a neighbor or two, or a hundred. We sought God and delighted in his ways yet served our own interests. We fasted and drew near to God but oppressed those around, beside, and below us. We humbled ourselves but bickered and fought with strangers. We abstained from food, but we didn't share it with the poor or those in need. We resisted consumerism but walked past the homeless man with holes in his coat. We sought God but forsook our neighbor. We pursued God but persecuted others. Our worship became a vehicle for wickedness. Our spiritual formation become a catalyst for selfish practice.

Like the ancient Israelites before us, many of us have lost our way with these disciplines. In fact, we could even say that many of us have lost ourselves in these disciplines. We've gotten a bit off track with how, why, and when we practice them. We've been searching for "fixes" that these disciplines will never be able to provide. We've come up short. We've been searching for experiences that

God won't provide on demand. This has been disappointing and maddening. The real danger, though, is not that we have practiced them in this way, which sets us up for failure and maybe even a crisis of faith because we never get the results we want. No, the real danger, as we see from this passage in Isaiah, is what we have done to our neighbor in the process. Or a better way of putting it: the real danger is what we have neglected to do for our neighbor in the process. While we have been trying to love God, we have been harming our neighbor.

This "vertical" dimension to spiritual disciplines may be news to you—and I hope *good* news—but it is only one side of the equation. This emphasis on spiritual growth and intimacy with God is only one part of the whole. And at least to God, it seems that it's not even the most important side of the equation or the most important part of the whole. When we take a close look at the Bible and church history (and even our own experience), we see that there's another side to these disciplines that we've overlooked. There's another angle that we've never noticed in our practice of them. There's another dimension to their practice that we've never heard preached from the pulpit. There's another profile that we've neglected to see in our small group study of these disciplines and in the books that we've read or speakers that we've heard. Something important has been sidelined. And it's a very important thing to God.

Somewhere along the way the "horizontal" dimension to these practices has been overlooked, ignored, and forgotten. All along, a focus on the neighbor and the benefit that these disciplines have for one's neighbor have been sidelined. And the time is ripe for it to be retrieved, explored, and developed. As you will come to see through the pages of this book, for Christians before us, these disciplines were not primarily or exclusively practiced for the intellectual goods that they offer each of us as individuals. They were not really practiced for us at all. Rather, they were practiced for others. They were practiced to help and benefit others. They were seen as acts of love toward one's neighbor that bring life and health and vitality to the world. They were seen as practices that discipline us to positively impact our neighbor's livelihood and concretely change the conduct of the communities of which we are a part. They were seen as good things to do in shared spaces with others.

When we step back and consider spiritual disciplines in this way—that is, when we look at them from the side and pay attention to this horizontal dimension—we see more than a bunch of seemingly random and strange practices that help us get closer to God. What we see is actually a synchronized and systematic way of living that reforms basic, everyday activities. We see ways of liberating and healing our everyday activities of owning, thinking, eating, socializing, talking, working, and resting. We see a coherent and integrated way of life that we were designed to live and the way that God calls and commands us to live. We see everyday activities done in ways that are healthy and honor God. But most importantly, we see everyday activities done in ways that help our neighbor and heal our relationship with others (i.e., family, friends, strangers, and enemies), including other animals and the earth, and harmonize our world. In short, we see the way of Jesus.

The Christian life is not a life dripping with personal satisfaction or one of basking in feeling "positive." It isn't a life baptized in stimulation or excitement. It definitely isn't a life of consecutive "highs" and "fixes." Rather, it is a reformed and transformed lifestyle lived according to the Father's design, the Son's example, and the Spirit's guidance. It is a life of reconciliation, restoration, and renewal. It is a life of loving our neighbor as ourselves. It is a life of doing everyday activities such as owning, thinking, eating, socializing, talking, working, and resting in ways that demonstrate love of others and bring life to the world. And as we will come to see, this is precisely the life we live by, in, and through spiritual disciplines.

These seemingly random and strange practices are actually sanctified and renewed ways of doing everyday activities.

Maybe you are like I was and you've dropped out of the school of spiritual disciplines long ago and you're doing just fine. You see the relevance and value that these disciplines have for pastors, educators, or spiritual directors—people who take their relationship with God really, really seriously and have the time for such activities—but you, an "ordinary," run-of-the-mill Christian sitting in the pew, don't have the time or energy for them. You don't really need them. Praying and reading your Bible in the morning is good enough for you. Because let's be honest: these disciplines are way too inconvenient to fit into our schedules and practice, they've "failed" us many times, and to be quite frank, we don't really see the need or the urgency to practice them. We're not "commanded" to do them, they aren't changing the world, and we're still going to get to heaven. If this is you, I was there, my friend. I completely understand.

If the person I've described is you, then this book will help you see a larger project afoot that might give you more incentive to give spiritual disciplines another shot. In your busy life as a hairstylist, entrepreneur, actuary, or homemaker, I especially hope you give them another shot. Or if you've never practiced them before, I hope you give them a try for the first time. For as you will come to hear and see, spiritual disciplines are for disciples of Jesus Christ living in the world—not just the really devoted ones who want to escape it. They are for all disciples who want to follow their Teacher to the ends of the earth. They are for you and they are for me—human beings living hectic lives, not aspiring angels seeking heaven through death. They are for those of us who want to follow our Lord and Savior here and now and love our neighbor as we love ourselves.

In general, many of us tend to overlook or maybe even downplay how our personal spiritual formation impacts those around us. We know that God calls and commands us to love our neighbor, and on a fundamental level, we know that our relationship with God involves others. But maybe what we don't know or realize is that others are implicated in how we interact and relate to God. Our relationship to God is through and through a public matter. It is a worldly affair. Our relationship with God influences and impacts life and livelihoods all around us—whether or not we want it to. And I hope we want it to. The Christian life is about bringing all things under Christ and allowing the Spirit to convict us and guide us in everyday, mundane activities. The Spirit does this through spiritual disciplines that influence and impact those around us. A change in our owning, thinking, eating, socializing, talking, working, and resting habits and practices influences our neighbor's life and livelihood. She experiences and is enlightened to alternative ways of doing these things. This instructs and benefits her.

God hangs out in the trivial. Transformation waits dormant in the mundane. Our Savior's redeeming hand leaves no stone unturned, and his renewing gaze leaves no square inch unseen. His call to us as his disciples to follow him and live in him means worshiping him in *all* that we do. When looked at from the side, spiritual disciplines are not just different ways of doing everyday activities but sanctified and renewed ways of doing them. They are ways of living in God. Our sanctification and the renewal of all things doesn't drop from the sky but comes through the Father, the Son, and the Spirit remedying and renewing the daily, mundane activities and the relationships, practices, and institutions that are built on them.

ONE

SPIRITUAL DISCIPLINES
AND THE WAY OF LOVE

A long time ago in a land far, far away, a Christian monk wrote a book and dedicated it to a bishop.[1] The monk's name was John Cassian, and in this book were the notes he took from observing several Egyptian monasteries that he had visited. In his book, Cassian described to the bishop the daily life he encountered in these monasteries and explained why the monks did what they did. He organized his observations of their daily life around eight principal vices that prevent the monks from living the way that they ought to live, and he offers disciplines for them to practice to counter these vices. He made clear that the monks do what they do on a daily basis to fix or prevent these vices from growing in their lives.

We may not be all that familiar with this word "vice," but it's an important word in the Christian tradition. It comes from the Latin word *vitium*, which can have various meanings: fault, defect, blemish, imperfection, corruption, or wickedness. Our English word "way" comes from *vita*, which is in the same family as this word *vitium*. A vice (*vitium*) is a defective or imperfect way (*vita*) of doing something. It's the wrong way to engage in some sort of activity or the wrong way to behave. Another word that captures this idea is "malformed." A vice is a malformed way of doing something, a bad or evil (*mal*) way of doing something. Throughout this book I use the word "malformed"—not "vice"—to communicate the idea that, like these monks, we do some very basic activities the wrong way. We do them badly, and sometimes even evilly.

The eight principal vices that Cassian discusses at length are gluttony, fornication, avarice, anger, sadness, acedia, vainglory, and pride. The monks gorge in their eating. They are greedy in their owning. They are prideful in their thinking. They are lazy in their work. This is not how they should live. It is clear from Cassian's treatment of them that these eight principal vices (which give rise to other "offshoot vices") comprise a way of life. They are like a package—or we might say that they come in bulk. Each vice works together. There is continuity between them, with each vice playing off another or building on another: gluttony feeds fornication, and vainglory gives rise to pride, for example. Although all of them are bad, Cassian notes, some of them are more destructive than others. Some are easily expressed in everyday living and have more disastrous effects than others, which means that some are more difficult to control and uproot than others. Pride, for example, is more difficult to uproot than gluttony. It's easier to stop eating so much than it is to stop thinking so highly of oneself. Because each vice builds on another, Cassian notes, the monks have to combat them in bulk. In other words, they have to *live* differently, not just *do* a couple of things differently.

In a quite detailed exposition, Cassian explained to the bishop how these vices emerge in the monks' daily activities and how they can be fixed through certain "institutes" and "remedies" in the community. By "institutes" and "remedies" Cassian meant rules and

practices. So he essentially suggests that the community of monks—
or the monastery—take up certain rules and practices to help them
fix the malformed ways that they do daily activities. And they must
do this together as a community. Together they will observe rules
and institute practices so they can perform these activities in the
right way. The remedies that the monks practice to rid themselves
of these vices are what we nowadays call spiritual disciplines. They
practice silence, solitude, fasting and feasting, Sabbath keeping,
meditation, and simplicity. They change the way that they dress,
own, think, eat, interact, talk, work, and rest. Spiritual disciplines
will fix their habits and practices and get them living the way that
they should in community or in shared spaces together.

Growing up as a Protestant evangelical, I used to think that monks
(and nuns) make vows to cloisters to escape the world and enjoy
personal intimacy with God. Fed up with the impurities of the world,
they go away and hide in the far corners of the earth where they can
be pure and undisturbed by the inconveniences of life while they
wait for the Lord to return. This always struck me as rather selfish
and cowardly. "Must be nice to get away from the inconveniences
of life and annoying miscreants of the subway and enjoy the peace
and quiet," I thought to myself. But, as Cassian's observations make
clear, this couldn't be further from the truth.[2] Monks and nuns make
vows not to a *cloister* but to a *community*. And they do so not to *escape*
the world but to *enact* a different one. They commit to living with
others and to living differently with these others. They commit to
disciplining their daily deeds for their own sake and for the sake of
others. They take living in community very seriously—the way God
does, as we saw in Isaiah.

Now some of us may be thinking, "A long time ago in a land
far, far away is right! This is a monastic community! Cassian was
a fourth-century monk! He's talking about monks! To a bishop,
nonetheless! I'm a cashier at a grocery store. I don't live in the

desert. I haven't taken any vows. I don't live in an intentional community with others—I live in a six-hundred-square-foot apartment by myself! We're worlds and centuries apart. What could this even mean for me? What hath fourth-century Egypt to do with twenty-first-century El Paso?" Our lives may take different shapes and twists and turns, but the cashier and the cenobite, the hedge fund investor and the hermit, the nun and the nurse are not so different. As followers of Jesus, we are all called to the same thing: God and citizenship in his kingdom. We are all called to bring our whole selves and all aspects of our lives under the power and sway of our King.[3] We are all called to bring the little things as well as the big things under his rule. Like the ancient brothers and sisters before us, we are called to discipline our daily deeds, and we are called to love our neighbor as ourselves.

I like how Reformed theologian Klaas Schilder (1890–1952) put it:

> We must serve God, everyone in his own way, wearing either a leather apron or an academic gown—it does not make any difference. Everyone has to serve God, wearing rubber boots or carrying a gasoline can, having as emblem a hammer and sickle (these belong to us) or a painter's palette, rather than a censer as such. We have to serve God, everyone in his own place in the new God-created community.[4]

We can learn a thing or two about discipleship and the discipline required of a disciple from our fourth-century monastic brothers and sisters. Like them, we do basic, ordinary activities every day. We get dressed, we buy things and take them home, we think, we eat, we hang out with friends, we talk (a lot), we work (a lot), and we rest. But what we don't realize is that we tend to do these activities in selfish and vicious ways. We do these things in ways that hurt our neighbor (and are unhealthy for us). And we are completely unaware of it because we have been doing things this way since childhood. And to top it all off, this way of doing things is unassumingly reinforced by culture and society—this is what everyone does and how everyone does it! But what the lives of these monks reveal to us is that we have to relearn how to be a human being and how God intended for us to act and live on a very basic human level. We have to relearn how to use our minds—not the mental faculties but the thoughts. We have to relearn how to eat—not the use of utensils but how much to consume. We have to relearn how to socialize—not to network for future jobs but to give people space. We have to discipline our daily deeds.

Disciplining Daily Deeds

As John Cassian rightly saw them, what we nowadays call spiritual disciplines are practices for a community to reform its way of life together—the thoughts, attitudes, habits, practices, and behavior of individuals, and the general lifestyle or way of living of the community. These practices are *for* a community as it interacts in healthy and harmonious ways in shared spaces. "We set ourselves against these struggles," Cassian said.[5] Notice the "we." This "we" is a company, not a collection of individuals. These monks saw themselves as a social body working together to weed out the vices that work against their communing and dwelling with one another. Together they disciplined their daily deeds. They improved their behavior for their own sake, as well as for the sake of one another. They fixed themselves for the community and their life together. It's pretty simple: in order to live in community and even to stay alive in community, we have to alter our lifestyle. We can't just do whatever we want to do. We can't just live selfishly. We have to be disciplined to some degree. We have to discipline our lives at least a little bit.

Many of us don't like this word "discipline." It makes us feel uncomfortable, even icky. It has negative connotations. We often associate it with punishment or retribution. To discipline is to punish, right? When a child does something wrong, we discipline him and send him to time-out. He sits in time-out as punishment for the wrong he committed. He has violated some rule in the house, and to make up for the "crime" we send him to time-out. And sometimes we tell him that he won't get a snack later. We are disciplining him; we are punishing him. To our contemporary mind, they are one and the same. But this confusion is unfortunate. Discipline and punishment are not the same thing. The root of the word "discipline" carries a much more favorable connotation than punishment. "Discipline" means instruction. To discipline is to teach, and to be disciplined is to be instructed. In meaning and practice, it is worlds apart from punishment. Whereas punishment is about paying a penalty or compensating for a wrong committed, discipline is about making things right. It's about getting back on track. It's about settling the matter. It's about resolving the issue. It's about fixing the problem. It's about healing a broken agreement or promise. It's about reconciling so that we can keep going.

The word "disciple" comes from this same root word. When Jesus says "You are my disciples," this means nothing less than that he is our teacher and we must learn from him. He instructs us in his way of life, and we implement it. He directs us in the way that we should go, and we go. He goes, and we follow him. But this implies that we aren't on the right path. We don't have it all together. Our way of living isn't right. To be discipled—to be a disciple—implies that we don't have it right. We don't have it figured out. We're doing it wrong. We don't know how to live in the way that our teacher wills and wishes, so we have to learn from him. We have to be instructed, corrected, and disciplined by him. That is what it means to call him teacher or master and for him to call us his disciples and followers. *This means that there can be no disciples without discipline.*

There can be no true image bearers without instruction. The endgame of following Jesus is not converts and confessors but citizens and custodians of his kingdom.

As many of us have come to see through years of following him, we have as many things to learn from him and from discipline in our lives as he has offices that he occupies and roles that he fills. Because Jesus is the firstborn of all creation and the second Adam, we must learn from him how to be a creature, a human being, and a son or daughter of the Father. Because he is our Savior and Redeemer, we must learn from him how to sacrifice our own agenda and live for others in love. Because he is our Prophet, we must hear the truth from him and learn how to witness to it in confidence and kindness. Because he is our Priest, we must learn from him to forgive others and intercede for the poor, the widowed, and the orphaned. Because he is the Judge of the world, we must learn to live more in tune with his ways and reign. Because he is our coming King, we must learn from him how to be citizens and custodians of his kingdom.

There is a trinitarian structure to be seen in our discipleship and the disciplining of our daily deeds. We learn from Jesus Christ how to take up and fulfill our original calling from the Father. As Christians, we believe that God the Father through the Son and the Holy Spirit created the heavens and the earth—a spiritual side to things and a physical side to things (Gen. 1:1). Both sides make up one creation, one world. Our world. Among all creatures, we human beings—because we have both a spiritual and a physical side—were called to cultivate, steward, and enhance this created order (Gen. 1:28). We were called to orient ourselves toward God and to bring all things given to our care and within our power under him. We were called to foster and contribute to making this world a place where God can dwell and his goodness and glory can shine. This is our calling as creatures, as human beings. And it has been ours since the beginning.

From the Son, we receive a new commission. Jesus singles us out, as his disciples, to follow and submit to him. He instructs us to learn from him and discipline our lives as he did and as we were originally supposed to do before things got out of whack (Gen. 3). He then sends us out into the world to baptize others and to teach them his way of life. He commissions us to teach his commandments and to make more disciples who will follow him (Matt. 28:16–20). He leads us to become renewed human beings in the world, to a life of doing everyday activities according to the Father's design, his example, and the Spirit's guidance, to a life of doing things in ways that liberate, empower, and enrich the lives of others and help creation flourish in wholeness and growth. Jesus challenges us to live a life of freedom through sacrifice. For it is through sacrificial living that we find life. It is in living for others that we find our life (Matt. 16:25; John 15:13; Col. 3:3–4), just as it is in him that we find ourselves. He reveals to us that we were made for something more than ourselves.

As we learn from him and live in him, we participate in a renewed creation and life in the Spirit, as he does. Jesus lived his life in, under, and with the Spirit. When we follow him, this is where he leads us, as the apostle Paul captures in his Letter to the Romans. Jesus does not lead us to reject the body (*soma*) or any other physical aspect of the created order, which the Triune God created good and Jesus redeemed. Rather Jesus leads us to resist living in fleshly (*sarx*) ways. He leads us away from sin and selfishness. He leads us to life in the Spirit. He invites us to bring our entire life under the guidance and direction of the Spirit, who is the power and source of life. Walk with the Spirit (Rom. 8:2–4). Be led by the Spirit (8:14). Think on the things of the Spirit (8:5–8). Let the Spirit change the way we behave (8:13), hope (8:23–25), pray (8:26–27), serve (7:6; 15:16), and love (15:30). Live in God and dwell in him. In Jesus we truly live life.

As Jesus showed, life is about bringing all things under the Father's reign through the power of the Spirit. It's about doing all things with, for, and in God. Sometimes we talk about a different aspect of our lives that we call our "spiritual life." But when we look to Jesus and really think about it, there is no distinct portion of our lives that we can call "spiritual" apart from everything else: the only choice is life in the Spirit or life in the flesh. There is no "spiritual life," there is only life in, with, and by the Spirit. God meant for every part of our life to be lived in tune with him who is Spirit (John 4:24). As his disciples, we learn from Jesus how to be creatures, human beings, who live by the power and guidance of the Spirit.[6] We learn how to live wisely, obediently, and responsibly, as God intended. We learn how to do everyday, human activities in the way that we were created to do them.

Spiritual formation is not just one component of our lives. It's not even one aspect of our lives. And it absolutely isn't one field of Christian study, separable from theology, ethics, psychology, or economics, for example. By the Holy Spirit, spiritual formation wholly forms all aspects of our lives into the image of Christ, who lived in, with, and through the Spirit (2 Cor. 3:18). It's about bringing all things human—our thoughts, attitudes, habits, practices, behavior, and lifestyle—under the power and sway of God, just as Jesus did.[7] It's about living in, and with, and for God, just as Jesus did. It's about doing and being all things human in ways that witness to God's kingdom and his purposes for all of life, just as Jesus did. And this is very, very important: spiritual formation—life in the Spirit—is about fixing the itty-bitty things of our lives so that they align with the rules, regulations, and rhythms of God's kingdom, just as Jesus did. It's about disciplining our daily deeds.

I hope that it's becoming clear to you that the way of Jesus is an intricate and integrated way of life. There is no disconnect between our call in Genesis, the commandments we are given in Deuteronomy, our commission in Matthew, and the new creation that awaits us in Revelation. Our original calling from the Father as human beings is tied to God's commandments to us as his people. These commandments are tied to Jesus's commandments and commissions to us as his disciples. These commandments and commissions, in turn, are tied to the Spirit convicting us and creating us into the image of Christ (Rom. 13:9). There is a coherence and consistency to the life that God intended for us to live. There are no gaps in the biblical story. There are no hiccups in God's plan or portrait. The creational, soteriological, and eschatological are one movement. There may be old and new in this story, but there is only one life and one plan.

Spiritual disciplines must be seen within this framework. They are not random and strange practices that someone indifferently invented long ago and that Christians have unquestionably practiced for centuries like mindless zombies. Rather, the disciplines are unique, alternative ways of doing basic, daily activities that Christians have deliberately practiced in order to change their lives. Now this is an important insight: these are not practices that we do in addition to our daily activities. Rather, they are alternative ways of doing things we already do. In fact, it would be best to see them as renewed ways of doing these things. As Cassian and others have made clear, each discipline attends to a different basic human activity and corrects a malformed way of doing this activity. For example, meditation renews thinking, fasting and feasting renew eating, solitude renews socializing, silence renews talking, simplicity renews owning, service renews working, and Sabbath keeping renews resting.

By correcting these basic human activities, spiritual disciplines lead us to live the way that we are designed to live. They are a synchronized and systematic embodiment of the way of Jesus. They are how he lived. They embody God's calling to us as human beings, his commandments to us as his people, his commissions to us as his disciples, and our now-but-future life in the new creation. Through them we open ourselves to the Spirit who sanctifies our lives and renews all life around us. Because these disciplines are a way of life, and each attends to a different activity, they need to be practiced in bulk, as Cassian and others have made clear. We can't just pick and choose one or two practices that we enjoy doing or find easy. If we're honest with ourselves and look closely at our daily deeds, we all could probably use some tweaking and correcting in our eating, thinking, sharing, giving, owning, resting, and working habits and practices. We could use a little bit of remedy and renewal in all the areas and activities of our lives.

For some of us, spiritual disciplines are very difficult. We're inconvenienced by them or we find ourselves in extreme discomfort in doing them. But this is not because we're doing something we've never done before but because we're doing differently what we've always done. We have been eating, thinking, sharing, giving, owning, resting, and working the same way for years. We've grown accustomed to doing things in this way. Change doesn't happen overnight. And there's an added layer of resistance because these disciplines are changing our selfish tendencies, which, if we're honest with ourselves, we don't really want to give up. The institutions of society and cultural practices have informed the ways that we eat, think, share, give, own, rest, and work. We have assumed that these ways of doing things are right and normal (i.e., the norm that we should follow), and we have just done them by rote. But that's the problem: they aren't right. And in God's kingdom, selfishness and harm to one's neighbor is never normal. This is precisely why *all* of us need to practice spiritual disciplines.

In the British crime drama TV series *Luther*, the main protagonist DCI John Luther (played by Idris Elba) asks a pointedly existential question for any Christian who cares about living wisely, obediently, and responsibly, witnessing to the way of Jesus in the world: "Don't you ever worry that you're on the devil's side without even knowing it?" This remark captures something important about the nature of sin: it likes to hide itself in our routine. It likes to work behind the scenes and never get any recognition. Sin is shy like that, and so is vice.

When we really think about it, sin and vice hide in the banal moments of routine and mundanity. It is in our cobwebbed and dark, forgotten places of habit and routine, and in our default cultural practices and lifestyles, that we are the most selfish and self-centered. It is in our daily deeds that we forget we need Jesus (and need to love our neighbor). We spend so much time trying to discern the Spirit and follow Jesus in our moral principles and political policies that we forget that Jesus cares about the most basic habits of our everyday living. We forget that there is a Creator with a purpose for all things, including thinking, eating, talking, or owning. We forget that there is a Redeemer who is restoring and healing all things, such as thoughts, impulses, words, and pockets. We forget that there is a Sanctifier who is renewing and making space for God to dwell in all things—even the littlest things we do every day.

What did you think about most yesterday? Where did your mind turn? What occupied your mind? How did you eat? What did you eat? With whom did you eat? How much did you talk? To whom did you talk? What did you post on social media? How many people saw you? How do you think you came across to them? What did you do when you had downtime or time off from work? Where did you go? Did you see anyone in need? Did you ask to help? What did you do yesterday? How did you live? I may be more malformed in my talking habits and practices than you. You may be more malformed in your resting habits and practices than I am. My eating habits may be more malformed than my resting habits. Your working habits may need more correction than your resting habits. Be that as it may, both of us need fixing and healing in all these activities. We don't do them as sacrificially and lovingly as we could. We could do them better.

As I've seen in my own life, it's in the crevices and corners of eating, thinking, sharing, giving, socializing, owning, resting, and working where sin seeps in, sets up shop, and festers for years. It's in these most basic activities that we are the most malformed and destructive. It's in these things—the most basic and unassuming activities we do every day—where we are most blind to God and most selfish in our behavior but also where God wants to open our eyes and bring healing through our sacrifice. It's in these ordinary, everyday activities that our Prophet wants to speak truth, our Priest wants to provide absolution, and our King wants to rule.

Christian discipleship is so much more than rigorously holding to our token moral and political concerns such as sex before marriage, alcohol, obscene language, drugs, "profane" movies, sexual orientation, and voting for a particular political party. Jesus cares about so much more than this. He died for so much more than this. He showed us so much more than this. He invites us to so much more than this. Being a disciple of Jesus means not only having a perspective on abstract ideas or scenarios but also having a handle on our concrete practices and situations. Following Jesus means changing the way we do things every day at their most basic level. Learning from him means being obedient in the little things, being faithful in all things, and most especially, glorifying God and loving others in, and through, and with everything. To be his disciple is to be disciplined by the whole of his teaching and his way of life.

Living Love

The ultimate goal of the Christian life isn't a bunch of cheap thrills of the sacred or even living a "meaningful" or "fulfilled" life. Nor is it "being a good person" and correcting our behavior so that we can live in good conscience in the confines of our intimate, personal relationship with God. That's not the way of Jesus. Jesus leads us ultimately to himself, that is, ultimately to love. We are called to love as he loved. That is where we are found. That is our end. Yet we cannot love as he loved or love as he loves all on our own. So we love through his love by practicing his love. Through his love, we find the power and energy and motivation to love. His love carries our love. And since he is love, and our life is found in him (Col. 3:1–3), then our lives will be love and love will be our life.

The way of Jesus is a life of love. And what really and truly makes us identifiable as his disciples is our love and the way in which we love. We will be different because we love and because we love differently. We will love when the world doesn't. We will love when others can't. We will love with our whole being, and we will love in the most minuscule ways. We will live love, and our love will go above and beyond other loves. Christian love is different from other kinds of love because it loves in the most minute, mild, and minor ways. A Christian—someone who follows the way of Jesus Christ—is someone who loves with her whole being. Her entire way of living is love, as she learned from her teacher: "Love your neighbor as yourself" means to do everything in a way that is advantageous, not afflictive, to your neighbor.

> By this everyone will know that you are my disciples, if you have love for one another. (John 13:34–35)

> Beloved, let us love one another, because love is from God; everyone who loves is born of God and knows God. Whoever does not love does not know God, for God is love. God's love was revealed among us in this way: God sent his only Son into the world so that we might live through him. In this is love, not that we loved God but that he loved us and sent his Son to be the atoning sacrifice for our sins. Beloved, since God loved us so much, we also ought to love one another. No one has ever seen God; if we love one another, God lives in us, and his love is perfected in us.

By this we know that we abide in him and he in us, because he has given us of his Spirit. And we have seen and do testify that the Father has sent his Son as the Savior of the world. God abides in those who confess that Jesus is the Son of God, and they abide in God. So we have known and believe the love that God has for us.

God is love, and those who abide in love abide in God, and God abides in them. Love has been perfected among us in this: that we may have boldness on the day of judgment, because as he is, so are we in this world. There is no fear in love, but perfect love casts out fear; for fear has to do with punishment, and whoever fears has not reached perfection in love. We love because he first loved us. Those who say, "I love God," and hate their brothers or sisters, are liars; for those who do not love a brother or sister whom they have seen, cannot love God whom they have not seen. The commandment we have from him is this: those who love God must love their brothers and sisters also. (1 John 4:7–21)

There is no getting around it: love is the essence of the Christian life. It's the X factor, the secret ingredient, the magic potion. Of all things that we are called to as disciples of Jesus Christ, we are ultimately called to love. Of all the characteristics that might define us as we follow Jesus, love will stand out most of all. Jesus tells us that love will be the most prevalent and persistent of all the qualities that define us. While we may categorize, identify, and evaluate others (even other Christians) on their political policies or moral principles, the Lord of nature and history—the one who sees and knows the future—tells us that the world will recognize us by something else entirely: our love.

As Christians, we take our understanding of love from Jesus's words and actions. We rely on him to know what love truly means and looks like. If there is anything that is clear to us in Jesus's words and way of loving, it is that he sacrificed for others. And through his sacrifices, he healed, liberated, and empowered others. His life of love and sacrifice led him straight to the cross. The ultimate expression of his love was his willingness to die for others. He did what he said was the greatest expression of love: he laid down his life (1 John 3:16). As his disciples, as those who are called to follow him and learn from him, we are called, commanded, and commissioned to similar action: "You shall love the Lord your God with all your heart, and with all your soul, and with all your strength, and with all your mind; and your neighbor as yourself" (Luke 10:27).

We all know that loving our neighbor involves sacrificing for her (Matt. 5). When she hits us in the face, we don't hit her back but turn the other cheek. When she takes from us, we offer her other items to take. When she makes us go far, we go even farther. When she begs, we give. When she wants to borrow something, we let her do so. If she is our enemy, then we must pray for her. We are called, commanded, and commissioned to give things up for her, such as our coat or maybe even the cup of water that we were about to drink. It might even come to dying for our neighbor. But the sacrifice we see in Jesus goes deeper than this. Jesus not only died for others; he lived for them. He laid down his life for them. And he did this every day he was walking through town, not just when hanging on that tree at Golgotha. His sacrifice was to lay down every aspect of his waking life for others.[8] This was his life's project: to live for others and not against them. When we look at his life and hear him speak into ours, we don't see or hear him invite us to live in a way that is selfish or self-centered. Rather he constantly invites us to sacrifice for others and to let him sanctify and renew our everyday living. He invites us through the Holy Spirit to live a life of love toward our neighbor.

This is much more difficult than it seems. Dying for another person is quite easy in comparison to living for another person. And living for a loved one is much easier than living for a stranger. Yet Jesus did both, and he calls us to do the same. Every day we do seemingly insignificant things. We sit down at the dinner table. We reflect on our day during the bus ride home. We chat with a stranger at a party. We call our mom. We finish an overdue report. Such simple, normal activities. Many of these things Jesus did, too. But we may not realize the ways in which we oppress, ignore, or neglect our neighbor through these activities. We're so focused on ourselves and doing these basic, mundane activities that we don't give any thought to how we're doing them and how the way in which we're doing them impacts those around us.

If we look closely and read between the lines, Jesus did these basic, human activities differently. He didn't do them in self-centered and selfish ways. He didn't use his words to malign others but to edify the adulterer (John 8:1–11). He didn't hoard his resources but shared meals with the sick (Mark 2:13–17). He socialized with the oppressed (Matt. 9:9–13). He gave to the hungry (Matt. 14:13–21). He ate, thought, shared, gave, owned, socialized, rested, and worked in ways that concretely and specifically loved his neighbor. It's commendable that we help out at the soup kitchen on Friday nights, set up for church on Sunday, and pray for a friend at the midweek Bible study. But how do we live the rest of the week? What do we do in other areas of our life? How do we love others with the other activities we do? What about other aspects of our living? What about the other "parts" of our minds and bodies? Is our entire life, our entire body, in the service of others: our meditation, silence, simplicity, fasting, feasting, Sabbath, and solitude?

What do we do with our heads and thoughts, tummies and urges, tongues and words, shadows and presences, pockets and possessions, hands and work, and bums and rest? Do we use them to love others the rest of the week? Do we live for others with these things too? Do we love others through our basic human activities? We may not live in a cloistered monastery, but we all live in some kind(s) of community—we all live in shared spaces. If we

FIGURE 1.1

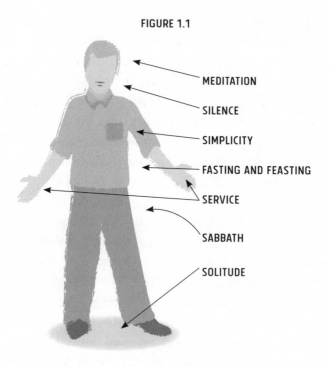

MEDITATION

SILENCE

SIMPLICITY

FASTING AND FEASTING

SERVICE

SABBATH

SOLITUDE

pay close attention to the circumstances and conditions in these shared spaces, we will see that our neighbor's livelihood depends to some degree on how we think, eat, talk, socialize, own, work, and rest. How we do these things has bearing on our daily life with others. But more importantly, we can love our neighbor in, with, and through these things.

We can either lift ourselves up with our daily deeds, or we can love our neighbor through them. We can either do them selfishly, or we can do them sacrificially. We can either help others with these activities, or we can harm them through ignorant, negligent, or oppressive ways of doing them. We can either positively impact our shared world with our neighbor, or we can negatively impact it. We can either do these things in ways that benefit us, or we can intentionally, strategically, and creatively do them in ways that are advantageous to our neighbor. This may sound like a ridiculous dream, but I believe we can love our neighbor and bring life to the world through simple changes in our habits and practices. By tweaking and correcting the way that we do everyday activities, we can concretely and substantively change the social, political, economic, and ecological landscape of our neighbor's life and our shared world together. By doing simple things like disciplining our daily deeds, we can bring healing and reconciliation to our relationship with our neighbor—who may be a parent, spouse, lover, friend, colleague, or stranger. We can love our neighbor in the itty-bitty moments and movements of our lives. This is what Jesus did, and this is what Jesus calls us to do. This is how we really, truthfully follow him.

When seen in this way, that is, from the side, spiritual disciplines should not be viewed as special practices for spiritual elites such as pastors, Christian educators, or spiritual directors. Rather they are valuable and vital practices for all believers and for our shared life in the world. They are sanctifying and healing practices for us as image bearers, disciples of Jesus Christ, and agents of the Holy Spirit who want to love our neighbor through the everyday things that we do. Christian, you don't need a powerful position or a deep pocket to love your neighbor. Jesus had neither. You don't need to go serve the poor in Calcutta in order to love your neighbor. You don't need a start-up company, a book contract, a speaking gig, a primetime interview, or an annual mission trip to love your neighbor. To put it crudely but truly, you can love your neighbor from the comfort of your own home. In fact, if you want to love your neighbor at all, you must change the way that you do everyday things at home (and elsewhere). If we want to love our neighbor and follow our Savior, then we must change the cobwebbed and dark, forgotten places of our general way of life. We must change the way that we eat, think, share, give, own, socialize, rest, and work.

As I unfold the horizontal dimension to these practices in the following chapters, the chart below will come in handy. It juxtaposes our typical view of spiritual disciplines with the horizontal view that I want to retrieve and develop. It's meant to expand our horizons and help us see the larger program of these disciplines.

CONTEMPORARY CHRISTIAN VIEW	A HORIZONTAL VIEW
Spiritual disciplines are for one's own benefit.	Spiritual disciplines are for the well-being of one's neighbor.
Spiritual disciplines are emotional or intellectual remedies for spiritual problems (e.g., doubt, despair).	Spiritual disciplines are behavioral remedies to basic human activities (e.g., eating, resting, working).
Spiritual disciplines inspire or edify believers in their faith.	Spiritual disciplines reform believers' mental and bodily habits.
Spiritual disciplines are a collection of individual practices from which one can choose.	Spiritual disciplines are a way of life that one must adopt as a whole.
Spiritual disciplines are practices that must be integrated into one's existing schedule and lifestyle.	Spiritual disciplines are developed out of one's existing practices, schedule, and lifestyle.
Spiritual disciplines need to be practiced only temporarily or seasonally.	Spiritual disciplines need to be practiced regularly and daily for the rest of one's life.
Spiritual disciplines are special practices that are distinct and separable from mundane activities.	Spiritual disciplines are alternative ways of doing mundane activities in which we honor the Father, learn from the Son, and follow the Spirit in executing these mundane activities.
Spiritual disciplines are done by individual believers.	Spiritual disciplines are done by individual believers, the institutional church, and other communities out in the world for the renewal of culture and society.

Side Steps: Spiritual Disciplines as a Way of Love

At the end of each chapter you'll find a section called "Side Steps." "Side Steps" plays on my horizontal discussion of spiritual disciplines and the importance of seeing them from the side. In these closing sections I offer two things: (1) a prayer particular to a given practice that you can pray during the week you are reading the chapter and (2) simple suggestions for practicing the spiritual discipline treated in that chapter. Ultimately these "Side Steps" are meant to get the wheels turning so that *you* can determine how best to love your neighbor through the everyday things you do. Treat these suggestions as guides, not guidelines—recommendations, not rules or regulations.

Prayer

Father God, you have created us with awareness, purpose, and insight. Through the prompting of the Spirit, grant us moments in our busy schedules to call attention to our lives. Through the instruction of your Son, give us the strength and honesty to examine and assess where we have gone wrong and lived selfishly. Give us the power to change our unhealthy and harmful habits so that we may live with integrity, charity, and service—for the honor of your kingdom and the well-being of our neighbor. In Jesus's name we pray. Amen.

Foundational Questions

As you begin to discipline some of your everyday practices, refer back here frequently and ask yourself these foundational questions:

- How exactly do I benefit my neighbor with my eating, thinking, sharing, giving, owning, socializing, resting, and working? Are some ways I do these things better than others?
- What tendencies, habits, inclinations, or impulses do I have when I am doing these activities? Are any of them "bad"? Why do I think I have these? Is anything fostering them or forcing me to continue them?

- Does this discipline require significant effort? Why is that? Am I trying to do too much? Is there something I'm unwilling to give up?
- In my day-to-day schedule, what prevents me from changing the way that I eat, think, share, give, own, socialize, rest, and work? What makes it difficult? What would make it easier?
- Are there other "second-tier" activities in my life that I may need to correct? Dressing? Playing? Commuting? Hosting? What would it look like for me to change these activities so that they are less self-centered and more neighbor-centered?

TWO

"WHAT DO YOU HAVE THAT YOU DID NOT RECEIVE?"

SIMPLICITY AND RENEWED OWNING

Once upon a time, there was a Greek philosopher whose father worked in the banking business.[1] Though he was no wolf of Wall Street, apparently he had a little bit of money. When this Greek philosopher was older, he went into the banking business, just like his father. After some time, unfortunately, there was a bit of a scandal and the philosopher lost everything. He was accused of wrongdoing, and the punishment that he faced was exile from his hometown. Things couldn't have gotten any worse—except that they did. As the story goes, eventually this philosopher was captured by pirates and sold into slavery.

Diogenes of Sinope (ca. 400–ca. 325 BC), aka Diogenes the Cynic, aka Diogenes the Dog (no relation, I think, to the West Coast rapper Snoop Dogg, aka Snoop Doggy Dogg), lived radically, and some would say crazily. The things that others thought were indispensable for life in society, he didn't. He tested the boundaries and limits of survival and need. With no place to call home or rest his head, he ate and slept anywhere he could. He was famous for being a hobo and a beggar. Probably because of what had happened to him, he came to despise money and sought complete independence and freedom from material goods. Legend has it that his only possession was a large tub that he rolled around and crawled into at night—it was his sleeping quarters.

Because he was known for living such an austere and crazily simple life (among other things), another famous Greek philosopher named Plato (ca. 429–ca. 347 BC) allegedly referred to Diogenes as "Socrates gone mad." The Athenians thought Diogenes's lifestyle was out of control. It was radical, reckless, even ridiculous. He was literally mad for trying to live in the manner that he did. Diogenes, however, didn't live that way for mere amusement or fame. He believed with conviction that the ancient Greeks had malformed practices of owning—acquiring, possessing, and consuming resources. They had become addicted to artificial and superficial things that actually made people vicious and unhappy. So Diogenes made a statement by living differently. He lived simply to show that people were living wrongly.

What hath ancient Greece to do with contemporary North American democratic society, you might ask. A lot, I think. While we might say that Diogenes himself had malformed practices because he didn't own anything, we shouldn't be too quick to judge. Like the ancient Greeks whom Diogenes critiqued, perhaps we too have malformed practices of acquiring, owning, and consuming. How often do we buy more than we need? How many of us have maxed out our credit cards? How many of us are in debt? Don't we buy things thinking they will please us and then never use them? How many items in our refrigerator perish because we have so much that we don't get around to eating all of it? How much do we waste each week? How many things do we own that we don't use?

We all own something. Owning is basic to being human and living in a society with some form of economy. We acquire, possess, and consume things all the time. These are daily activities for us. And like all things human, owning is done in community and with the help of community. What we acquire, possess, and consume most likely comes from someone else's hand. We don't make our own laptops, cereal, silverware, shirts, and cars—someone else does. What we create or make or do on a daily basis may reach someone's hands, or others may benefit from our owning it. The TV one roommate owns can benefit everyone in the apartment, if he shares. How we own and what we own is shaped by the resources and creative ingenuity of others. And, conversely, how we own and what we own informs and affects those around us.

If we take an honest and close look at how we own—if we take a worm's-eye view of how we acquire, possess, and consume things—many of us will agree that our owning habits and practices tend to be selfish and malformed. We tend to own in ways that covet and make our resources for our own benefit and enjoyment only. More often than not, we tend to be possessive of our possessions. To some degree, when we do this, we hurt our neighbors and negatively impact their livelihood. Although our possessions seem like minor things, they affect those inhabiting shared space with us. We can tell that this is so when we look at our neighbor's attitudes, expectations, and circumstances.

Malformed Owning: Living Lavishly

Once upon a time, there was another Greek philosopher. This philosopher lived shortly before Diogenes. He was very famous—more famous than Diogenes—and Diogenes himself was a huge fan. This philosopher went by the name of Socrates (469–399 BC). Socrates was so (in)famous that poets wrote poems mocking him, philosophers wrote dialogues "starring" him, and early Christians claimed him as one of their own. In fact, some of these early Christians even referred to him as a "Christian before Christ."[2] Now that's saying something! Socrates inspired many generations, especially with his remarks at his trial before the Athenian pantheon: "The unexamined life is not worth living."[3] Socrates liked to examine his life, which is what Diogenes liked so much about him. Socrates lived an honest and integrated life. He constantly examined his life to determine if he was living in a way that was right and would bring him happiness.

One time Socrates was having a conversation with a man named Glaucon. They were discussing what it takes to make a just city. They were thinking along these lines: "What if we started all over again and were able to build a city from the ground up? What would it take to make this city just? What would it take to make this city good? What would we have to do to get the people to live rightly—as they should—and help them find happiness? What kind of education would we need to institute? In general, what sorts of things could we do without?" Long before they got to the kind of education that they would need to make the citizens learn and value good character, they began discussing what everyone would need in this city. Certain material goods and resources would be essential to make such a city. Socrates began by saying that food, shelter, and clothing would be all the people really need to survive.

Glaucon scoffed at this notion and told Socrates that they were building not a "city for pigs" but one for human beings.[4] Glaucon claimed that having only food, shelter, and clothing was too austere and simple for human beings. You might as well put them in a sty and throw in some mud. Glaucon believed that human beings need more refinements and comforts than food, shelter, and clothing. If anything, those are the assumed basics. They are the essentials of the essentials, but human beings need much more. Glaucon then started to enumerate to Socrates these essential amenities. Some of them were the equivalent of couches, tables, delicacies, cosmetics, courtesans, actors, poets, and gold and silver. Glaucon's argument was that human beings *need* these things. We cannot and should not get rid of them.

At the heart of this discussion is a deeper, nuanced conversation about the nature of luxury (*luxus*) and lavishness (*laute*). Is there a difference between living comfortably and living excessively? Or are they one and the same? Is it possible to live comfortably without living excessively? Or must we own more than we need in order to do so? Can we find luxury in having nothing? Can we find luxury in living simply? Or related to this, does living elegantly require us to live extravagantly? In order to be stylish, sophisticated, and dignified—characteristics befitting a human being and not a pig, according to Glaucon—do we have to own a lot of really expensive stuff? Or can we find elegance in simplicity and even austerity?

Lavishness is extravagant or elaborate living. It is to live beyond one's means. We live lavishly when we acquire and possess material resources and goods in excess. It is when we take too much and own too much. We take more than we need; we take more than is necessary for us to survive and even to live comfortably. When we live lavishly, we take well beyond what is befitting for us and meets our needs. Because we take beyond our means, lavishness often results in hoarding, which we can see if we look closely at the lived practice of the lavish person. The lavish person acquires and accumulates so many goods and resources beyond his needs that he cannot or does not use all of them. There is just too much for him to use, so he has much left over.[5] He doesn't usually give it away, so more often than not, these excess resources go to waste while the lavish person continues to acquire.

Perhaps we consume to excess because we get satisfaction from looking at the breadth of what we have: "Wow, look at all these great things I have!" Maybe we do it out of a competitive spirit: "God helps those who help themselves!" Maybe we need the security that comes from having a ton of stuff on which to rely. Or maybe more perniciously, we do it because we want others to be jealous, envious, or covetous. But living lavishly doesn't have to be a grand affair. For many of us, living in excess doesn't express itself in extremities. It doesn't translate to tying $4,000 to balloons and releasing it into the air. It doesn't have to amount to owning six houses (two of which we never use) and four Rolls-Royces. Excess comes in petite sizes, too. Maybe we need a comfortable pair of sneakers because we're on our feet all day at work. Instead of just getting a pair from a trusted brand, we walk out of the mall with three pairs of Air Jordans. Lavishness is unique to each of us in our own position and means of living.

Lavishness is not a type of owning—that is, it's not a true representation of owning—but a malformed way to own. It is not the way Jesus owned, and it doesn't seem to be the way that Jesus calls, commands, and commissions us to own—because it's a selfish way to own. We can and should love our neighbor with our pockets and wallets, but we are not doing so when we live lavishly and hoard. To buy more than we need when our neighbor is most likely living in poverty is not to love our neighbor with our pockets. To hoard and waste material goods and resources when our neighbor is in need is not to love our neighbor with our wallets. Living lavishly and hoarding disregard our neighbor and ignore her situation. How are we loving our neighbor when she is suffering and we are living sumptuously? How are we loving our neighbor when she is picking up crumbs and we are living in a costly fashion?

Malformed Owning: Squandering Wealth

There are three very basic aspects to owning: acquiring or spending, possessing or having, and consuming or using. Lavishness, as already mentioned, is a malformed way to acquire and possess things. It is the wrong way to do the first two acts of owning. Squandering is another malformed way to own, and it's a selfish way of doing the third aspect of owning—consuming and using things.

The Bible tells us that everything we have is a gift from God (1 Chron. 29:11–16; Ps. 24:1; Eccles. 5:18–6:2; 1 Tim. 6:17). Nothing is technically ours—it all traces back to God and something he has done to make it possible for us to have anything. Our house on the plot of land that we bought—God's (Lev. 25:23). The jewelry in our drawer—God's (Hag. 2:8). "Charlie," our Labrador—God's (Ps. 50:10–11). All these things are technically God's. Every good and perfect gift (James 1:17), including life itself (1 Cor. 6:19–20), is from God. All our possessions are gifts from God that can and should be used for constructive and helpful purposes. They should be conserved or preserved and used toward the best possible end.

To squander is to consume or spend these possessions recklessly and foolishly, as if they weren't gifts from God. The one who squanders uses his possessions without any consideration for his future conditions, his present circumstances, or the well-being or circumstances of those around him. He throws his gifts away or wastes them. Or at the very least, he doesn't use them to their full potential. That is, instead of using them to remedy a problem in his present circumstances or help others in theirs, he makes poor, selfish decisions and uses his resources for lousy ends—such as his mere enjoyment. Typically we talk of money being squandered. But many more of our possessions can also be used recklessly and foolishly. For example, we can squander our food, time, energy, and even our thoughts.

If we look closely at our experiences with squanderers, we can see that squandering and lavishness often go hand in hand. The one who lives lavishly—that is, the one who owns in excess—owns so much that he can and does use some or all of his possessions recklessly and foolishly. He has so many resources that he can afford to just throw some or all of them into the wind as if they were nothing. He doesn't care about how he uses his resources because he doesn't have to care—he has so many of them! Anything that he squanders he can just replace. Squandering isn't really a big deal to him. He has so much that he can spare a few frivolous purchases or bad decisions.

Squandering is not a type of owning but a malformed way to own. It is not the way that Jesus used his resources, and it isn't the way that Jesus calls, commands, and commissions us to use ours. Like living lavishly, squandering is a selfish way to own. We should love our neighbor with our pockets and wallets, but we are not doing so when we squander our resources. To use foolishly and recklessly what God has given us to help others is not to love our neighbor with our pockets. To make our possessions primarily and exclusively the means for our own enjoyment or personal satisfaction is not to love our neighbor with our wallets. Squandering puts us in a position where we do not love our neighbor with our possessions and resources as much as we could. It is to throw her out of the equation. How can we love our neighbor when we don't give her anything or bless her with anything we own? How are we loving our neighbor when we blow our money on frivolous things and she is begging on the street? How are we loving her when we recklessly go through our resources and she is rummaging through garbage cans?

Simplicity and Renewed Owning

I was standing at the bottom of the stairs when she said it.

"Dave, take him over there and sign him up." As she spoke, she gave him the eye.

The bottom right corner of my dad's mouth always drops when he knows better. It's like his wisdom-tell. When he complies, against his better judgment, it bounces back up and goes back to its rightful place. It doesn't take years to notice it—any Joe Schmoe can see it, and most Joe Schmoes know my dad to be a wise man. He kissed my mom, and he and I walked out the door.

Roberta—his navy-blue Chevrolet van that he used for installing carpet six days a week—was just a few yards away. She was on the brink of reaching that fifty-thousand-mile marker today. My dad was eager for that day. In fact, this day was probably the day that she did. We hopped in and buckled our seat belts. Today she had a distinct aroma—she smelled of dried glue, fresh plastic, and a hint of banana Life Savers.

Keys in the ignition, my dad exhaled and turned toward me.

"You really want to do this?" He exhaled again. I felt the weight of what he was asking and what I was hoping for and requesting. Reluctantly, and with guilt, I whispered to my dad, "Yeah, I think so."

He turned Roberta over, and we drove away.

That spring Saturday morning just before 11:00 a.m. in Fairport, New York, my dad spent his last sixty dollars for the week so that I could play spring baseball. Little League. His last sixty dollars for me to play a sport that only the families of the players attended. My dad gave the last sixty dollars he had to a naive, self-centered ten-year-old boy who didn't see beyond his present desires and reputation. Yet this dad gave.

Among other things, my parents taught me the importance of sacrifice. I saw them sacrifice firsthand because they sacrificed for me. I saw them give and share what they owned and at a time that was certainly not opportune. And yet they gave. I saw how it affected them because it affected me, too. We lived on powdered milk, ramen noodles, and hot dogs for the week. (Have you ever tried powdered milk? Don't.) It wasn't until years later that I realized that my parents had showed me something much more—something that I had overlooked for most of my childhood: living simply.

Putting Simplicity in Perspective

We often misunderstand the nature and purpose of simplicity. That is, we misunderstand what simplicity is as well as why someone would practice it. The popular misconception is probably that practicing simplicity is a lot like the way Diogenes lived, as we encountered at the beginning of this chapter. We typically think of it as giving away everything we own or losing it. We barely have a place to call our own, we don't always have food to eat, and we might even sleep somewhere strange now and again. It either means we are a hobo forced out into the streets to beg, or we are some kind of progressive or hipster who goes out into the woods to live more deliberately.

Let's clear the fog. First and foremost, simplicity is not a renunciation of material goods. Living simply doesn't mean that we have to reject material goods and condemn those who have them. We don't walk away from societal living and give up comforts and refinements. Living simply doesn't cash out to withdrawal from these sorts of things like asceticism does. Simplicity does not require asceticism, and asceticism doesn't necessarily follow from simplicity. They are two distinct modes of living. Nor does simplicity have to lead to a life of poverty. Living simply and living poorly are two distinct sets of circumstances. To live simply doesn't mean that we are constantly in a state of need.

Sometimes we confuse simplicity with frugality. Frugality is another term associated with owning. A frugal person is someone who makes wise decisions with money and food. "He is frugal in his spending," proud mothers sometimes say of sons who use their chore money wisely. Simplicity is akin to frugality in that it involves being economical and thrifty in owning. People who practice simplicity are often frugal with what they have. However, simplicity goes beyond frugality in one important sense: simplicity is a lifestyle, and frugality is an act. Frugality is a way of acting that can be applied to any lifestyle, but simplicity is a lifestyle that results in frugal actions. A lavish person could certainly be frugal with his resources and use them very sparingly, even stingily. But the one living lavishly cannot live simply. For that would be living the exact opposite of how he lives. To live simply is not to live lavishly.

On its most basic level, simplicity is a way of life. It is not simply an act or a practice but a way of living within one's means. Particular acts and practices of simplicity are demonstrated, but they emerge from the more basic lifestyle being lived. The one who lives simply is oriented in his acquiring, possessing, and consuming by what he needs to survive, and maybe just enough to live a tad bit comfortably. It's about not owning too much or even too little. One who lives simply doesn't go beyond his means of living. He doesn't get, keep, or use more than he needs. He lives with what he can and must use. He lives within his means, and that's all. He owns just what he needs for his own unique circumstances and conditions. In other words, he lives simply within his context and not his neighbor's. Simplicity is simplicity for him. But no matter what, there is no excess for him.

Loving Our Neighbor with Our Pockets and Possessions

Those of us brought up in the Christian tradition probably weren't introduced to simplicity as a distinct spiritual discipline. We may have heard of it, but we never really associated it with spirituality or identified it as a spiritual discipline. Yet we probably inferred from passages in the Bible, such as Acts 2, that it's a good practice for us: "All who believed were together and had all things in common; they would sell their possessions and goods and distribute the proceeds to all, as any had need" (Acts 2:44–45). What we probably didn't realize or hear preached from the pulpit is the value of practicing this discipline in contemporary culture and its horizontal benefit. By making slight adjustments to our habits and practices of owning—our purchasing and consuming—we can help our neighbor and maybe even bless her.

A few years back I became acutely aware of the economics of everyday living. My wife, daughter, and I had just relocated to New Jersey from Los Angeles, and we were about to be greeted by a very disgruntled Hurricane Sandy. My wife and I headed out to the store to stock up and brace ourselves for this Category 3 hurricane. When we arrived at our local grocery store, there were no jugs of water or batteries for flashlights. We tried another. And another. And another. Alas, nothing. Everywhere we went, all we found were people standing in customer service lines inquiring when the next shipment would arrive.

When Sandy struck us in 2012, it flooded our city. We lost power—well, except for two blocks: ours and the one just north of us. I remember going outside our building to check out the damage on the streets. I pushed our building door open to see about thirty people assembled around the stoop. A couple of baby strollers were in the mix. I looked left and right to see that our first-floor neighbors had hung power strips out their window so that neighbors could charge their phones. They had also baked cookies for them to nibble on as their phones charged and they called family. That year I realized that in a very concrete and practical way, our owning habits and practices affect other people inhabiting shared space with us. This might occur on a minuscule scale, but it is nonetheless significant. How we acquire, possess, and consume resources directly impacts our neighbor and her livelihood.

When we take jugs of water off the shelf at the grocery store in preparation for a hurricane, our neighbor can't take those jugs off the shelf. When we clear out batteries from endcaps at the home improvement store in preparation for a natural disaster, others have to go without, maybe a day, maybe a week. Regardless, this will affect our neighbors and their livelihood for the next few days, weeks, or maybe more. When we live lavishly and take more than we need, we dominate the resource pool. We take from our neighbor.[6] When we hoard items, we keep goods that our neighbor needs. When we squander our money or possessions, we use things foolishly and recklessly that our neighbor could use and might cherish and use wisely. We need to think about this. On a concrete, everyday basis, our acquiring, possessing, and consuming habits and practices affect our neighbors and their livelihood in significant ways. When we take, we take from our neighbor. When we own, we own what could be our neighbor's. This may seem insignificant *to us*, but it's definitely significant to our neighbor.

Owning is a good thing. We acquire, possess, and consume material goods and resources so that we can sustain our lives, live comfortably, and even enjoy these goods. We own to live. There's nothing wrong with owning. The problem is not that we own but how we own. We have to consider how we acquire things and how much we acquire. We have to think about how we possess things and how tightly we hold them. We have to be aware of how we consume things and how we use them. Do we acquire, possess, and consume in selfish ways? In what ways does our owning come at the expense of our neighbor? Does it directly or indirectly oppress and marginalize her?

Medieval Dominican friar Thomas Aquinas (1225–1274), in his commentary on the Lord's Prayer, specifically the fourth petition ("give us this day our daily bread"), points out several ways that our owning habits can become selfish and sinful.[7] His discussion helps put things in perspective. He says that we become selfish and sinful in our owning when we (1) want things beyond our state and condition of life, (2) abuse and defraud others in our acquisition of these goods, (3) are never content with what we have but must have more, (4) consume or spend too much in a day when it could last for many days, and (5) become proud in our possessions and forget that they come from God.

At the heart of this discipline is the idea that we are part of one household: God's creation. Our lives and our possessions are given to us to be stewarded and shared with others. Our pockets and wallets have something in them so that we can share with others.[8] God calls, commands, commissions, and convicts us to give to others what he has given to us. He doesn't give things to us so that we can hoard them or hide them from others. He makes it possible for us to own so that we can bring life and love to others. He blesses us so that we can bless those around us. We are supposed to use our wallets and pockets for his glory, not our own. Our economy is meant to correspond to the divine economy in which the Father, the Son, and the Holy Spirit live, share, and give.[9] As those made by, made like, and made for God, we are meant to receive and give and share like he does.

Whatever intellectual or material goods we think are ours are derived from God and will one day be cast before him (Rev. 4:10). In a sense, they are on loan to us. He gave them to us, but one day we will give them back. He has deputized us to steward these gifts, not squander them. He has called us to love others through them and with them, not hoard them or live lavishly with them. We hear this consistently in the New Testament: "In all this I have given you an example that by such work we must support the weak, remembering the words of the Lord Jesus, for he himself said, 'It is more blessed to give than to receive'" (Acts 20:35). "Do not neglect to do good and to share what you have, for such sacrifices are pleasing to God" (Heb. 13:16).

We live in a society of exponential industrial productivity and technological development. We make a lot of things, and we tell ourselves that the possibilities are endless. We believe that we will one day have an indefinite supply of everything. In such a society of productivity and development, it's easy to deceive ourselves. It's easy to mistake fantasy for reality. We forget that this world is finite and limited. The truth is that there isn't an infinite supply of things, just a vastness of opportunity and goods that we find overwhelming and inspiring. Despite all attempts to make it otherwise and to change these conditions, we do not live in a world of unlimited resources—natural (i.e., water) or artificial (i.e., cars). Plants wither. Pickles spoil. Animals go extinct. Water is contaminated. Toys go out of stock. Food becomes scarce. Funds become insufficient. Apartments are in short supply.

This world in which we live with limited resources is a world shared with others. We are not the only ones living in this world. We share a pool of resources and material goods with our neighbor. When we pluck an apple from a tree, another one doesn't instantaneously blossom forth. When we go the grocery store and clean the shelf of cookies, the grocer may not have another case in the back. Items run out. Resources are depleted. Others have to wait. Our neighbor might be deprived. In such a world, it's very important to conserve, preserve, and steward what we have. In such a world, people who live with only what they need are very valuable and useful.

In such a world—one that also includes corporate bonuses, multiple homes on the shore, and several wine cellars—the practice of simplicity is an act of love toward our neighbor. It resists selfish owning. It leads us to discipline how we acquire, possess, and consume things in our world. It gets us to ask: "Do I really need this, or do I merely want it?" "Can I live without it?" This leads us to be conscientious and modest in what we purchase and own. We learn prudence in consuming and what we really need to survive. It gives us the opportunity to be generous in giving away those possessions that we won't ever or don't ever use. Simplicity remedies and renews our selfish habits and practices of owning. It disciplines us to live within our means and to own only what we need—not more than we need (prosperity) and not less than we need (poverty).

Because simplicity works off the needs of an individual, a household, and a community, the practice of it must be contextual. We have to be sensitive to who we are and what we are capable of doing. What counts as simple living will look differently depending on one's age, gender, quality of life, conditions of living, and so forth. In community, each of us will have to discern and discover what simple living looks like for us. In other words, the practice of living simply for a start-up social media millionaire will look different from simplicity for a blue-collar carpet installer with three kids. Simplicity for a professor will look different from simplicity for a professional athlete. The needs of the community will also play a part.

Although we are talking about simplicity as a practice, it's actually a lifestyle. In fact, it is the edifice upon which all the other spiritual disciplines discussed in this book rest. This is why I have treated it first. While simplicity deals primarily with owning, it informs all the other activities that we will discuss. The other disciplines feed off simplicity. Simplicity is the trunk of the tree of discipline, and the other disciplines are the branches.

Many of us give to charities and parachurch organizations, our local congregation, and maybe even the homeless man on the street. This is all great and commendable. We should continue these acts of giving. But then we let our wallets continue to fatten and our pockets to overflow, as if it didn't matter. We're not aware of our owning habits and practices. We don't challenge our desires and purchases. We're aware of how deep-pocketed conglomerates can ruin neighborhoods, but we are oblivious or indifferent to the ways that we hurt our neighbor with our wallets and pockets.

If we truly want to love our neighbor as ourselves, then we need to change how we buy, possess, and use things every day. For most of us, we simply need to share and give to our neighbor. We don't do that enough. We need to love her with what we have, yes, but we also need to love her by refraining from acquiring things we don't need and won't actually use. That is another way to love her. We aren't really loving her as ourselves if we keep everything to ourselves. One small but significant way that we can do this is by altering our daily deeds and everyday owning so that we are deliberate about how and what we acquire, possess, and consume. Consistently and frequently living like this would help us love her on a much deeper level.

Side Steps: Simplicity

Prayer

Father God, the world you created is full of life and possibility but limited in resources and possessions. You have called and commanded us to be content and prudent. Through your son, Jesus Christ, teach us how to find peace, joy, and comfort in taking little and giving much. Through the power of the Holy Spirit, counsel us in how to live simply. Convict us to help those in need. Give us compassion for those who are in need. Grant us the courage to give when we need. Comfort us and protect us if our giving puts us in need ourselves. All for your glory and our neighbor's good. Amen.

Simple Steps to Practice Simplicity

- Pay attention to your purchasing habits. Do you buy in bulk? Are you an impulsive buyer? When do you feel the need to shop? If you buy in bulk, try getting only stuff for the week. Through trial and error, see how much you really need in a given week. If you're an impulsive buyer, stay away from the things that ignite that impulse. If you know what makes you feel the need to shop, try to resist it in a constructive and healthy way. Go for a run or call a friend who can keep you accountable for your purchasing habits.

- How often we take out the trash is a sign of how much we use and consume and perhaps of how much we waste. Keep a record of how often you take out the trash. Mark it on the calendar, if that works. If you see an irregular pattern, and it's not because you were away on vacation or hosted a party, then that's a good sign that something is awry. In our household, that usually means that we combed through the fridge and disposed of a lot of spoiled food. These exercises help us rethink how often we need to purchase those items.

- Walk around your home, room by room, item by item, and ask yourself, "When's the last time I used this?" Depending on the object, if you haven't used it in a while, it might be something that you don't need. Give it to someone who could use it.

- Sometimes we deceive ourselves and tell ourselves that we need more than we do. As a community (household, business, youth group, sports team), we should practice simplicity—not simply as individuals. Family, small group members, close friends, and even, to some extent, next-door neighbors can help us discern our needs. If you're serious about it, muster up the courage and ask them: "Is there anything in my life that you think I don't need?" "Is there anything that I have that you might need?"

- Use "spring cleaning" or however frequently you clean your apartment or house to examine and evaluate how you can live simply. Every year I end up purging inessential books that I'll never read again and donating clothes that no longer fit. Frequent exercises in purging can help us live simply.

++++++++++
THREE
++++++++++

DIRECTIONS FOR RULING THE MIND

MEDITATION AND RENEWED THINKING

Like every college professor I know, twice a year I simultaneously anticipate with curiosity and dread those digital, shrill cries that students send out at the end of the semester with the click of a button. I get kind of nauseous opening them, but I seem to always relish reading them. "Professor, I'm not going to be able to submit the assignment on time. Can I have an extension?" "Bennett: I'm not going to be able to make the final exam as scheduled—can I take it at the end of the week?" Then they submit their reasons. Usually they are quite amusing.

Fall semester of 2015, however, things took a bit of a different turn. I received two emails from different students informing me that they would be at a funeral and wouldn't be able to submit an assignment on time. Admittedly, I was a bit suspicious. Two students, unrelated to each other, going to the same funeral? Pfft. Yeah, right. But my heart sunk below my knees when I saw the pictures and RIPs on social media and eventually watched their tears fall on my office desk a few days later. It was sobering and disheartening.

That very morning I heard on the news that an adolescent boy had "tragically died." When that newscaster reported the story, she said something newscasters sometimes say at such a time: "Our thoughts and prayers are with the family." We do a similar thing when tragedy strikes our world. When a friend or a loved one (perhaps even a stranger) shares such devastating news, we typically say, "Oh, I'm so sorry" or "My condolences." Sometimes we say, "I'll be thinking of you" or "You and the 'fam' are in my thoughts and prayers."

"I'll be thinking of you." "You're in my thoughts." Why do we say these things? What do we mean by them? Do we mean anything by them? Regardless of why we say them, doing so brings great benefit to those who hear them. The afflicted feel supported. The suffering feel comforted. The victimized feel loved. When we say these things to them, they know that we are thinking of them during this tragic and unfortunate event, and that means something to them. Our thoughts of them count for something.

Thinking is basic to being human and functioning as a human being. We calculate, judge, deliberate, imagine, and wonder every day. These are common activities for us. And like all things human, thinking is done in community and with the help of community. Others have helped us learn how to think, and others continue to help us in our thinking. Middle school math teachers taught us how to calculate. College philosophy professors (hopefully) taught us how to deliberate and wonder. Grandfathers taught us how to imagine. How we think and what we think about are informed by the thoughts and thinking of others. And, conversely, how we think informs and impacts the lives of others.

If we take an honest and close look at how we think—if we take a worm's-eye view of how we judge, deliberate, imagine, and wonder and about what—many of us will agree that our thinking habits and practices tend to be selfish and self-centered. We tend to primarily, or even exclusively, think of ourselves and no one else. Our thoughts are flooded with concerns for our own well-being, and our heads are filled with thoughts of ourselves. In fact, we tend to think that our heads are ours and what we do in and with them is our business. I want to single out two selfish tendencies in the thinking habits and practices of North American democratic culture that I believe, to some degree, hurt our neighbor and negatively impact her livelihood. Although selfish thinking might seem a minor thing, and therefore harmless, it can hurt our neighbor and negatively impact life in community with her.

Malformed Thinking: Being Self-Absorbed

One way that we tend to be selfish in our thinking is by being self-absorbed. Most of us probably don't think evilly about our neighbor. We don't think about killing her. We don't think about eradicating her name from the annals of history. We don't ponder spitting on her grave. Sure, *thoughts* like these may occasionally come to mind, but we don't entertain them. We don't dwell on them. We just brush them to the side and move on. No, for many of us, our problem is that we probably don't even think of our neighbor. We are too busy to think evilly of her. We are too busy to think of her at all because we're preoccupied thinking about ourselves.

To be self-absorbed is pretty self-explanatory: it happens when our thoughts are exclusively oriented toward ourselves. When we are self-absorbed, we always have ourselves on our mind. The self-absorbed thinker, though, is someone who actively does this. He isn't only swallowed up by himself and his concerns. Rather he is so engrossed in and consumed with himself and his daily tasks and responsibilities or reputation that he intentionally orients his thoughts toward himself, even when he knows that to do so is to ignore, overlook, or neglect others. Others are not only not on his radar, but he makes sure this is so. In other words, the self-absorbed thinker actively tries to be absorbed with himself.

But self-absorbed thinking doesn't have to be deliberate and ill intentioned. It can be accidental and innocent. For example, the college professor immersed in writing and working during the academic year can forget to get his wife a wedding anniversary gift. Or the young entrepreneur speeding to catch the ferry into the city can be oblivious to the homeless man hoping for breakfast every morning. The homemaker can be so concerned with finishing the piles of laundry and doing the dishes that she neglects to play with her kids and shouts at them for disturbing her.

Whether self-absorbed thinking is intentional or accidental, we are so consumed by our own matters and concerns that we forget that others matter and that their matters matter too. "Yet we are mindful, though not as yet awake" to use a line from American poet E. E. Cummings (1894–1962).[1] We are thinking, all right, though not about others. We are mindful, all right, but not awake to our neighbor. We are mindful of ourselves—very mindful—but we are not yet awake to the presence and needs of those around us. We are acutely aware of ourselves and all our needs, but we are in a deep and pathological slumber with respect to our neighbor. Our neighbor isn't even on our radar because there isn't any room in our head for her. She can't enter our thoughts because there are too many thoughts in our head about us!

Self-absorbed thinking is not a type of thinking—that is, it is not a true representation of thinking—but a malformed way to think. We can't get into his head, but this doesn't seem like the way that Jesus's mind worked, and it doesn't seem to be the way that Jesus calls, commands, and commissions us to think. It's a selfish way of thinking. We can and should love our neighbor with our heads and thoughts, but we are not doing so when we are self-absorbed. To always be thinking about ourselves is not to love our neighbor with our heads. To always be concerned about ourselves is not to love our neighbor with our thoughts. Self-absorbed thinking disregards our neighbor. It ignores, overlooks, and neglects her. How can we love our neighbor when we don't even think of her? How can we love her when we're distracted and don't pay attention to her? How can we love her when we forget her birthday, don't invite her to the birthday party, or fail to notice her at the party? How can we love our neighbor when we are absorbed with ourselves?

Malformed Thinking: Thinking Maliciously about Others

Another way that we tend to be selfish in our thinking is by thinking maliciously of others. The word "malice" derives from *mal*, which means "bad." In its most basic definition, malice is wishing something bad to befall someone. It is to hope and long for someone to experience evil.[2] It is when we think evilly about our neighbor. We think about her losing her job or her spouse dying. These thoughts don't just occasionally come to mind; we make them come to mind. And when they do, we entertain them. We feed them. We water them and let them fester and grow.

Whereas self-absorbed thinking is to overlook our neighbor because we're always focused on ourselves, malicious thinking is to think evilly about our neighbor out of some consideration for ourselves. We are not too busy to think of our neighbor—we make it our business to think of her and to think of her in an evil way. Our motivation for doing so is usually rooted in something that we don't like about our neighbor in comparison to ourselves. She looks better than us. She does something better than us. She thinks "better" than us. She did something to us that we don't like—even something insignificant such as stealing our parking spot during rush hour at the mall.

Malicious thinking, however, doesn't have to involve hatred. Malice and hate are not the same, and they aren't always conjoined. To think maliciously of someone, you don't have to hate that person. You don't have to despise her to imagine and entertain the thought of her downfall. You don't have to passionately detest her. Whoever is on the other end of your malicious thinking doesn't have to be someone you hate; it could be a random person who gave you the stink eye on the street. And it doesn't have to result in spending five years plotting to hurt him; it can be simply frequently and consistently thinking evilly about him. Thoughts will come and go, but malicious *thinking* is at work when we deliberately provoke, entertain, and feed the frequent and consistent holding of wrong or wicked thoughts about someone.

Malicious thinking does more harm than we think. We can't think about our neighbor's downfall one day and then the next day imagine her success and prestige. Our heads don't work that way. Our thoughts are more ingrained and forceful than this. Consistent and frequent thinking about our neighbor's downfall or just thinking evil thoughts about her affects us as whole persons and our interpersonal life with her.[3] If we feed these thoughts, they will grow into attitudes and feelings. Our evil thoughts, imaginings, and memories will shape our living with our neighbor. Animosity and hostility will build up. This, in turn, will influence our behavior toward her the next time we see her. Whole persons cannot so easily divide their heads and thoughts from the rest of their being.

Malicious thinking is not a type of thinking—it is not a true representation of thinking—but a malformed way to think. While we cannot get into Jesus's head, malicious thinking doesn't seem consistent with who he is and what he calls us to do with our heads and thoughts. Like self-absorbed thinking, malicious thinking is a self-centered way of thinking. To always be thinking about hurting our neighbor is not to love her with our heads. To always be thinking of our neighbor's wrongs and how wicked she is, is not to love our neighbor with our thoughts. Malicious thinking is the wrong way to think of our neighbor. We can't truly or genuinely love our neighbor when we think ill of her. Love is not longing to hurt someone or thinking about their suffering. We do not truly love our neighbor if we do not love her with our heads, and we cannot truly love her in other areas of our lives when we are frequently and constantly thinking ill and evilly of her.

Meditation and Renewed Thinking

At the heart of French philosopher René Descartes's (1596–1650) works was a frustration with competing truth claims about the world and reality. Descartes was alive during the Thirty Years' War and saw firsthand how conflicting convictions can lead to suffering and strife. "Everyone can't be right," he thought. Some must be right, and others must be wrong. Either the Catholic Church is right, or the Protestant church is right. Either Plato is right, or Aristotle is right. They can't all be right. Yet they seem so persuasive! Why do they have so many adherents if they are wrong? Fed up with these options and the continued conflict that they brought, Descartes proposed completely starting from the beginning. What if we were to doubt everything that we've been told by our parents, the church, our teachers, and our friends and start from scratch? What if we carefully used our own reason—and didn't take Plato's or our professor's or our pastor's word for it— and came to our own conclusions? Well, that's just what Descartes did. Or tried to do.

Using what he called the "natural light" of reason as his guide, Descartes doubted everything he could about the world and himself until he was satisfied that he had reached something that couldn't be doubted—something that would be the bedrock of certainty. He needed something from which he could begin his knowledge. From there, he would start building up his knowledge of himself and the world. The story goes that Descartes did indeed find what he sought. In his most famous work, *Meditations on First Philosophy*, he claims that there are two things of which he could be certain: that he exists and that God exists.[4] He and God were realities that he could not doubt. In his other work, *Rules for the Direction of the Mind*, Descartes gave his readers the "inside scoop" on how he reached this certainty and a manual for how they could do so too. He proposed a simple—to him—but rigorous method for using our heads to discover true and undoubtable knowledge. All we need to do is follow his twenty-one rules (a few more were planned, but the work was never finished).

Descartes firmly believed that if we are to know the truth, we can't just arrive at it by fumbling and stumbling in our inquiries. We have to know what we're looking for in order to discover it. And we have to be "equipped," if you will, to receive it. For him this meant that we have to know how to think on a very basic level and we must be able to make good judgments about what is true and false. Though his *Rules* is quite technical, he probably saw it as a kind of "how to fix your head" manual. Now if we lay aside what we think about Descartes's confidence in the modern scientific ideals of his day (namely, that there is a step-by-step method to discover all truth about the world) and also lay aside what we think of his aspirations (that we can be *certain* of things, whatever that means), a very basic claim emerges: there is a right way to think about the world and know the world, and our thinking can go awry. But there are ways to get our thinking back on track.

Putting Meditation in Perspective

After Moses passed away, God gave Joshua these instructions:

> This book of the law shall not depart out of your mouth; you shall
> meditate on it day and night, so that you may be careful to act in
> accordance with all that is written in it. For then you shall make
> your way prosperous, and then you shall be successful. (Josh. 1:8)

What does this mean? What is meditation? What does it mean to
meditate? What was God instructing Joshua to do? Why was this
important to God after Moses passed? In what sense does meditation lead to acting according to the law, as it says here?

There are quite a few common misconceptions about meditation.
Some people don't even know what to make of it, like Ron Swanson
(played by Nick Offerman) on the NBC comedy series *Parks and
Recreation*. After visiting a meditation center, Ron says, "All told, we
were in there about six hours, and no, I was not meditating. I just
stood there, quietly breathing. There were no thoughts in my head
whatsoever. My mind was blank. I don't know what the hell these
other crackpots are doing." Perhaps the most popular misconception
is that meditation is a sort of absent-mindedness or some kind of
"empty-mindedness." It is a time when we shoo away bad thoughts
or pressing concerns and focus on being alive or becoming aware
of life. We do it to be at peace.

Meditation is not a lack of thinking, but instead it is a form of
thinking—thinking in the sense of having and "using" thoughts.
Rather than being a lack of thoughts, in the biblical sense and in the
Christian tradition, meditation is an orienting of one's thoughts.[5] It
is the act or practice of directing one's mind and thoughts toward
something. Even for the one who believes that meditation is emp-
tying the mind of thoughts, when they're shooing thoughts away
during meditation, what are they doing but directing their minds?

Consciousness is always oriented toward something—that is to say, we are always focused on something in our world even if we are not aware of it or concentrating on doing so.[6] Our mind does it for us, so to speak. We can understand meditation as taking consciousness by the hand and leading it somewhere to say, "Pay attention to this!"

When we meditate, we concentrate, we focus, and we orient our mind toward something. "Meditate" comes from the Greek word *medesthai*, meaning "to care for," and from the Latin word *meditari*, meaning to "consider," "think over," or "measure." This gives us a broader perspective for grasping the essential features of meditation. What makes meditation unique among other forms of thinking is that meditation allows us to measure or weigh something over an extended period of time. We focus on it, and we take in its value and worth. It is a lengthy, investigative, and focused mode of thinking. Our minds are directed for an extended period of time. We consider the thing or "see" it from all angles. As we're "looking" at it and thinking about it, we measure its weight, depth, complexity, totality, value, and significance. If we get distracted, we're constantly bringing our attention back to the thing and "holding" it before us.[7] We're concentrating on it. We "stare" at it, if you will.

Other forms of thinking include calculating, deliberating, discerning, imagining, wondering, contemplating, and judging. Meditation is one type of thinking among these others. And what we do through meditation differs from these other movements of the mind. For example, whereas calculation, judgment, and deliberation are more oriented to solving a problem, meditation is oriented toward awareness and enjoyment—we can meditate on a math problem, but we don't meditate to solve a math problem. Whereas imagination tends to pull something apart and play around with the pieces, meditation considers something in the integrity and purity of its presentation or revelation. It considers the thing as the thing is given. Whereas wonder stands back in awe and appreciates something, meditation passionately investigates the something and gets lost in it.

Loving Our Neighbor with Our Heads and Thoughts

Those of us brought up in the Christian tradition were probably taught that the spiritual discipline of meditation involves contemplating God's words (Josh. 1:8; Pss. 1:2; 119:97). This usually means pondering the hidden truths of the Bible—"I wonder what this passage *really* means"—and waiting for God to mysteriously reveal hidden truths to us. Sometimes it is prompted by crises, but many other times it is just the thrill of learning. We enjoy growing in our knowledge of him. We're titillated by new insights or different ways of seeing what has been given in his revelation of himself and his plan for the world.

There's nothing wrong with thinking about God's words and the deep truths at root in them, of course—this is something we must do. This is how we come to know God on a deeper level. We hear what God has said to us. We listen to what God tells us about himself and what he's done for us. Nevertheless, I think that we've reduced this discipline to what it affords us and overlooked something important in our practice of it. Meditation offers more than what we can get from God or how we can draw closer to God. We tend to miss the horizontal dimension of this practice. We miss that meditating on God's Word involves thinking about our neighbor.

Six out of the Ten Commandments that God gave us deal with our neighbor (Exod. 20:12–17). Let's bring that down to size a little bit: If God spoke only ten times, six of those ten times he would say: "Don't do that to your neighbor." Only four times would he say, "Don't do this to me." Do you think God cares more about how we treat our neighbor than how we treat him? Or do you think that we have more opportunities to mistreat our neighbor than we do to dishonor him? However we look at it, apparently God cares about how we interact with and treat our neighbor. Obviously he wants us to consider our neighbor and her well-being.

If that's not enough to convince us, the apostle Paul makes it abundantly clear:

> For the whole law is summed up in a single commandment, "You shall love your neighbor as yourself." (Gal. 5:14)

One law: love your neighbor. Essentially that's what everything is about. That's the one thing that God tells us to do. We are to love our neighbor. And we are to love her in particular ways and in particular things. But how can we love someone we constantly forget? How can we be concerned for someone who doesn't capture our attention? How can we care for someone who eludes our concentration? In order to love our neighbor, we have to remember, consider, and think of her.

Technically, when we meditate on God's Word (and particularly his law) day and night (Ps. 1:2), we are meditating on our neighbor. Or we should be. How can we meditate on God's law and not ponder our neighbor? How can we consider the Ten Commandments without focusing on the six of them that deal with our neighbor? How can we call to mind God, his story, and his calling to us without orienting and directing our mind toward our neighbor? If our meditation on God's law is to actually be a meditation on God's law (and not what we want to ponder and consider), then our time of meditation must include some consideration of our neighbor.

At the heart of meditation is the idea that we as whole persons belong to God—bodies and minds. Our desires and our thoughts belong to him. Our hands as well as our heads are his. He is the Creator, Redeemer, and Restorer of all these things. And he calls, commands, commissions, and convicts us to steward these gifts in ways that lift up and love our neighbor and heal and harmonize our world. We are supposed to use our heads and thoughts for his purposes, not our own. They are not truly ours, and we ought not to treat them as such. They were made to help us seek the advantage of others (1 Cor. 10:24). They were made so that we could regard others as better than ourselves and seek the interests of others and not our own (Phil. 2:3–4).

Our minds were made to know the truth—to know God and his ways. They were made to understand the reality of our world, God's design for it, and God's view of the things that he has made. With this comes the truth about our neighbor—that she is created in God's image, she is redeemed by his Son, and she is comforted and convicted by the Spirit.[8] She is not our nemesis. She is not a competitor. She is not an alien. She is a fellow human being. She is an image bearer. She is a child of God. And we should see and think of our neighbor as Christ does.

If we grow up thinking of our neighbor as a selfish miscreant, we will consistently and frequently see our neighbor as a selfish miscreant. This, in turn, will shape how we treat and respond to her. When she steals our parking spot at the mall, after we have thrown a few obscene gestures at her, we will tell ourselves that she's just a selfish miscreant who needs Jesus. We have ingrained it in ourselves through brief but continual thoughts time and again (or maybe extensive contemplations) that she is an evil person. These thoughts have shaped our response to her when she wrongs us or inconveniences us.

But if through our meditation we are consistently and frequently reminded that our neighbor is someone who is broken, disoriented, and caught up in the selfish ways of the world just like we are, we will be less likely to throw obscene gestures at her and tell ourselves that she has it out for us. If we are reminded that she is "fearfully and wonderfully made" by God (Ps. 139:14), we will be less likely to think of her as a selfish miscreant. If we are reminded that quite possibly she is or could be our future sister in Christ, we will be less likely to judge her. If through our meditation we are regularly reminded that God loves her and we are here to love and serve her, we will be less likely to let our anger, frustration, and exasperation get out of hand.

When we are busy entertaining nasty thoughts about our neighbor, or ignoring her, or are too consumed with ourselves to think about her, we aren't using our minds in the way that God called, commanded, and commissioned us to use them. We aren't loving our neighbor as we can and should. We are using our heads and thoughts in broken, rebellious, and idolatrous ways to tear her down, hurt her, and offend her. Some of us may have great jobs that invite us to or demand that we use our minds to help our neighbor. We might be architects who build condominiums and skyscrapers so that our neighbor can have a home and an office. Or we might be teachers who educate the next generation of neighbors. Or we might be entrepreneurs who lay out business plans for a new app that will be convenient and affordable for our neighbor's consumption.

But *using our mind* for our neighbor and *thinking of our neighbor* aren't the same. We need to be mindful of our neighbor. In the hustle and bustle of our lives, we lose control of our heads and our thinking. Often we're not even aware of what we're thinking. We just go through the motions, and our thoughts are everywhere. When we try to collect them at the end of day, we can't seem to find them because we weren't aware of them in the first place. More often than not, our thoughts were concerned with ourselves and our benefit.

We could use some direction in our thinking. We could use some discipline in our heads. We need a rule to direct our minds so that we can control our thinking and thinking patterns. We need a way to become more aware of others and their well-being. We could use something to help us remember our neighbor, especially in our daily deeds. The discipline of meditation is exactly what we need. It's about thinking of our neighbor. It's about being reminded of her. It's about thinking healthy and good and true thoughts about her. It's about correcting unhealthy and wrong and false thoughts about her. It's about learning to love her in our heads so that we are reminded or motivated or mindful to love her in the rest of our livelihood.

Meditation is a practice that remedies and renews selfish thinking. It is a practice, not simply an exercise. It is not something we do to better ourselves; rather it is a way of acting and doing (*praxis*) things in the world. It's something we should do every day. By taking time to meditate on God's Word, which we have already noted encompasses some form of thinking about our neighbor, we push back on the malformed ways of thinking that we discussed above. We stop being so self-absorbed. In a sense, just by turning to God we resist this self-absorbed thinking. And then our meditation on God's law and gospel prompts and convicts us to consider those around us: the poor, the widowed, the orphaned, the stranger, our enemies, animals, the forest, and the land on which we stand. In meditation, our neighbor and the importance of treating her well become the focus.

In a world where people inconsiderately use cell phones in libraries, talk in movie theaters, and leave their dog's feces on the sidewalk, wouldn't the daily practice of meditation be an act of love toward our neighbor? It would discipline our minds to turn toward our neighbor and consider her frequently and consistently—*at least* six out of ten times. It would remind us of her and of what God thinks of her. By meditating on God's Word, we are constantly brought face-to-face with her worth and how we should treat her. This is sufficient reason to practice this discipline every day. We love ourselves every day—if we are to love our neighbor as we love ourselves, then we need to think of our neighbor every day. By making small adjustments to our daily habits and practices of thinking, we love our neighbor as ourselves. By making the practice of mediation part of our daily routine, we bring our neighbor and her well-being into focus frequently and consistently.

Being mindful of her will lead us to wonder how she's doing. It will lead us to imagine and deliberate about how we can help her in her current situation. It will lead us to see and interact with her differently. It would be quite difficult for us to love her with our time, energy, possessions, and the other basic activities we're going to discuss in this book if we weren't mindful of her. Thinking of her must be the foundation. Loving her with our heads and our thoughts is essential to loving her at all.

Do not underestimate the importance of being mindful of your neighbor. Many of us keep our pants on until marriage, abstain from drinking too many cocktails, go on diets, and respectfully decline drugs at a party. We beat our bodies into chastity and purity. We do all sorts of things to keep our bodies in check because we know that a person's body is a temple (1 Cor. 6:19), which is great. Yet we let our minds run amok and think rebelliously, as if doing so doesn't matter. We don't think about our thought habits and patterns. We don't challenge the thoughts that come into our heads. We are acutely aware of how we hurt our neighbor with our bodies—for instance, when we punch our neighbor or roll our eyes at our neighbor—but we are oblivious to the ways that we hurt our neighbor with our minds and thoughts. If we truly want to love our neighbor as ourselves, then we need to change how we think about our neighbor.

Side Steps: Meditation

Prayer

Heavenly Father, you created us with minds to attend, concentrate, wonder, conceive, imagine, reflect, calculate, understand, deliberate, examine, and judge. You sent your Son to renew our minds so that we could be transformed in how we think and how we envision the world. Invade our thoughts this day and steer them toward the truth of all things. Send your Spirit to prompt us to think of others and to keep our neighbor at the forefront of our minds. In Jesus's name we pray. Amen.

Simple Steps to Practice Meditation

- As appropriate and available, schedule fifteen minutes a day to meditate and think about your neighbor. As this time becomes more rhythmic and easy over the next days and weeks, try thirty minutes. Then try an hour. Remember, though, what is most important is consistency and regularity. If you can do it for only five minutes a day, make sure you do it for those five minutes every day.

- Depending on the time of day and what you are making, cooking can be a great time to meditate. While you are chopping and mixing, be deliberate about orienting your thinking. Reflect on the past morning or afternoon. Ponder your thoughts, attitude, behavior, and pursuits. How often did you consider your neighbor? Was there a time when you could have helped or loved your neighbor through something small?

- Do you have a long commute? Do you drive a lot? Instead of playing Spotify, listening to talk radio, or calling a friend (or, God forbid, texting!), take time to redirect your thinking. This can be a great exercise, especially if you are distracted by self-centered and nasty drivers on the road!

- Every morning while you're brushing your teeth or getting ready for the day, take time to pay attention to what consumed your mind yesterday. After getting into the habit of reflecting on the previous day, start to prepare your thoughts for what you're going to think about this day. Tell yourself to think about your neighbor. "Okay, Kyle, try to remember Miles today. How can you help him or love him this day?" After a few days, try to do this in the evening too. We retain things better if we think about them before bed.

- Is there someone at work whom you don't like or have trouble working alongside? Before bed, try to call to mind the previous day's events, and if your colleague did something right, appreciate this. Then ponder several good characteristics you can identify in this person. On your drive to work in the morning or your ride on the train, do the same. Imagine encountering this person during the next few hours. How could you set the tone for the day? What could you say? Imagine saying it. And then when you get there, do it.

- Read the Bible daily. See and hear God love and defend your neighbor in what you read. Write down passages that speak to you. To remember them, write them on your mirror. Put sticky notes on your desk or on the back of your front door. Try to see where God is at work in your neighbor. Where is she creative and productive? Appreciate these things. Where is she good and just in her life? Acknowledge these things. In what things is she intelligent and able? Admire these things.

FOUR

THIS IS MY TUMMY, WHICH I WILL CURB FOR YOU

FASTING AND FEASTING AND RENEWED EATING

Many of us give a lot of thought to what we eat and where we eat. We're lactose intolerant, so we avoid dairy products. We don't enjoy food poisoning, so we avoid hole-in-the-wall restaurants with "un-satisfactory" sanitation ratings. We know what we like to eat, and we know what we don't like to eat. We know where we are willing to dine, and we know where we would never take family visiting on Friday night. We spend a lot of time visiting WebMD and Yelp and reading online culinary reviews.

A few of us may have wondered why we eat, even though that seems like a nerdy way to spend a Friday night. It's pretty obvious why we eat, isn't it? To nourish ourselves! We eat for the sake of health, growth, and energy—duh! We eat so we won't die. Some of us eat to avoid getting irritated, upset, and antsy. Others eat to avoid walking around with migraines. We eat so we won't fall apart in public. We gobble down that Snickers bar when we're "hangry" at the game. When we're hungry, we sit down, open our mouths, and scratch that internal itch before it gets out of hand. We satisfy ourselves, and depending on our age, we've been doing it for some time.

But how many of us have ever thought about *how* we eat? Eating is basic to being human and necessary for human survival. We nourish ourselves with food and water every day. It's routine. And like all things human, eating is done in community and with the help of community. Many of us eat around others every day. We don't grow our own food, so we rely on farmers and grocers to provide the resources for the meals that we cook or bake. Some of us don't even cook our own meals but rely on mothers and fathers or chefs to make them for us. What we eat, where we eat, and how we eat depend on the eating habits and practices of others. Their habits and practices may even inform our own. Conversely, how we eat informs and impacts the lives of others.

If we take an honest and close look at how we eat—how we consume food, with whom, where, and what—many of us will agree that our eating habits and practices tend to be a bit self-centered. We tend to make eating primarily about our own nourishment and enjoyment. As some of us know from experience, the urges that emerge from this hidden, clawing abyss that we call the "tummy" lead us to be cold, nasty, and brutish toward our neighbor. I want to single out two selfish tendencies in our eating habits and practices that, to some degree, hurt our neighbor and negatively impact her livelihood. Although these might seem like trivial matters, we can actually wage a war against our neighbor with our waist, if we're not careful.

Malformed Eating: Gormandize

One way that we tend to be selfish in our eating is by being greedy or gluttonous.

In the movie *Se7en* (1995), Detective Summerset (played by Morgan Freeman) and Detective Mills (played by Brad Pitt) arrive at a grisly crime scene: an obese man is seated face down in a plate of spaghetti with his hands and feet bound by barbed wire. A few minutes later, viewers are informed that this man was coerced to eat until he passed out and then booted in the belly until he hemorrhaged. Behind the refrigerator the word "gluttony" is written. Though a bit grotesque, this scene brilliantly captures the nature and consequences of gluttony: too much food, compulsion, some form of violence, a food coma, illness, and maybe even death.

We all like good food, and we enjoy eating these good foods, as we should (Eccles. 3:13). But enjoyment of good food is not the same thing as gluttonous eating. Gluttonous eating goes beyond mere enjoyment—all the way down to unhealthy indulgence. Another word for gluttony is "gormandization." The word "gormandize" comes from "gourmand," which is someone who enjoys good food . . . but enjoys it a little too much . . . and a little too often. To gormandize or to eat gluttonously is to eat too much and too often.[1] Not only does this result in obesity, illness, and possibly even death, but it also has considerable implications for the community in which one gormandizes.

Excessive indulgence is often related to greedy acquisition. Someone who eats a lot tends to take a lot. And when the gluttonous eater takes a lot, he monopolizes resources. Monopolization, of course, is not specific to food and eating. There are many other commodities that one can monopolize: cars, water, class time. Regardless of what market the monopolizer controls, he always treats himself as if he is the only inhabitant of his world. Quite literally, he lives as if he is the only (*mono*) citizen in his city (*polis*). He takes and consumes without any regard for others. He is oblivious to them, or he simply ignores or overlooks them. He doesn't care. Enjoyment and indulgence are his number one priority.

By frequently obtaining an excessive amount of goods and consuming them, the monopolizing eater dominates the pool of material resources. He controls the market on these goods. As we discussed in our chapter on simplicity, this has implications for those around him. When he takes, others can't. He consumes what others may want or need. This monopolization finds expression in our everyday living. On a very basic, micro level, a monopolizing eater could be someone who takes the last hot dog without asking, even though he has already had three. Or someone who carries around the bag of potato chips at the party and doesn't make them accessible to anyone else. Or on a more complex, macro level, he is someone who clears the shelf of his favorite beer at his local neighborhood market without any consideration of those in the neighborhood who share the same interest in this brand of brews.

Gluttonous eating, which typically results in monopolizing resources, is not exemplary eating. It is a malformed, selfish way to eat. As Jesus's life shows, we can and should love our neighbor with our urges and our tummies, but we are not doing so when we eat greedily and monopolize food or drink. Playing a board game (Monopoly) that encourages a strategic domination of a market is an amusing way to pass a Friday night with family or friends, but it's a very harmful way to relate to our neighbor the rest of the week. To put our enjoyment first is not to love our neighbor with our urges. To constantly pursue indulgence is not to love our neighbor with our tummies. How are we loving our neighbor when our comforts, more often than not, come at the expense of our neighbor's inconveniences and crises?

Malformed Eating: Miserly Eating

Another way that we tend to be selfish in our eating is by being miserly. As Langston Hughes's poem "Ballad of the Miser" clearly brings to the fore, a miser is someone who hoards wealth and spends as little as possible. As Hughes eloquently expresses it, the miser puts his wealth in a sock and stashes it away. The poem concludes with these lines:

> When he died he didn't
> Will a thing to anyone—
> To a miser saving money's
> Too much fun.[2]

He doesn't want to use it; he wants to collect it. He may even scheme and plan how he's going to save and where he's going to put it all. He enjoys doing so. Though he may have more than enough to spare, he doesn't want to throw down even a few dollars to buy some nice clothes, so he may even look like a beggar. All he wants to do is to keep stuffing and saving. In the end, he leaves nothing to anyone.

"Miser" comes from the Latin word for "wretched" (*miser*). I think we can understand this association in two ways. First, more often than not, the miser looks wretched. He goes "around in rags like a beggar would," as Hughes puts it. He looks like he's in bad shape because he doesn't spend any of his money. He doesn't fix himself up or maintain or adorn himself. Second, we could also understand wretched as applying to the miser's internal state. He is an irritable, frustrated, or angry person. He has likely always worried about how much he's earning and how much more he could be saving. He's in the wrong state of being. He's never right with himself. In short, he's unhappy. But that's kind of what we should expect, isn't it? Aren't most penny-pinchers rather curmudgeonly?

Recall our conversation earlier about frugality. The miser is very different from the frugal person. In the end, the frugal person is defined by his spending. He spends his money, and he does so wisely; he doesn't collect or hoard it. The miser, however, is defined by his lack of spending. He doesn't spend his money; he stores it up. He just collects and collects and collects. He is stingy with his money. He doesn't want to give it up—for anything. He would rather increase his stash than put a new shirt on his back. And unlike the frugal person, if the time does come when the miser spends his money, it doesn't necessarily follow that he will spend it wisely. He's not used to spending, so he could be fairly lousy at it.

Of course, miserliness doesn't apply only to cash. It can apply to food and eating too. A miserly eater might be someone who hoards food and doesn't consume it. He buys things not to nourish himself or to enjoy them but just to collect them. He refrains with all his might from sharing them, and he definitely doesn't give anything away. He is stingy with his good food and drink. An example of this stinginess in our culture is buying really tasty bottles of wine but never cracking them open. Or buying the best steak or fish on the market but not serving it when others are over for dinner. The miserly eater avoids consuming what he has and might even avoid being around his neighbor so that he doesn't have to share what he has. If friends or family come over for dinner, the miserly eater might offer them the subpar or inexpensive bottle of wine—for instance, the "Two Buck Chuck." Or he might encourage a potluck-style meal so he doesn't have to give up his stock. In the end, he doesn't want to share his expensive or quality stash with his neighbor because he values his stash more than he values his neighbor.

Like gluttonous eating, miserly eating, which often results in hoarding resources, is a malformed way to eat. Jesus cooked and shared his food with others (John 21:12–13). Unlike the gormandizer or the miser, Jesus didn't eat selfishly. Like Jesus, we can love our neighbor with our tummies and our urges, but we are not doing so when we eat like misers. This may seem trivial and insignificant, and therefore not as destructive as eating greedily, but on a very basic interpersonal level, miserly eating really hurts our neighbor.

If she knows that we are holding out on her or saving the best stuff for ourselves, this will affect how she interacts with us. She won't trust us. She won't associate with us. She may even hold a grudge. That's because no one likes to associate with someone who doesn't share—we learned this when we were toddlers.

Miserly eating betrays the debt and gratitude we owe to her and others for the resources we have and use to nourish ourselves. It fails to steward our gifts in a way that benefits and loves our neighbor. When we practice miserly eating, we do not share or give the good gifts that have been given to us. That said, I hope that we can see at this point how some of these selfish ways to own, think, and eat are connected and, eventually, how the disciplines of simplicity, meditation, fasting, and feasting work together to resist and remedy them. Acquisitive greediness can be rooted in living lavishing. Those who eat too much, take too much. Similarly, our monopolizing practices of eating that lead us to overlook others when we should be considering them can be rooted in our self-centered thinking habits. We are too concerned with our own enjoyment and indulgence to remember our neighbor. Selfishness is a way of life, but so is sacrifice.

Fasting and Feasting and Renewed Eating

John Cassian tells the story of a monk who would not eat when no one was around:

> We met someone else who was living in the desert and who testified that he never permitted himself food when he was alone. Even if for five full days none of the brothers stopped by his cell he would put off his meal until, on his way to church on Saturday or Sunday in order to participate in the devout assembly, he came across a stranger. He would bring him back from there to his cell and join in a meal with

him—not out of bodily need but for hospitality's sake and for the brother's own good.[3]

What does this story from John Cassian's travels in Egypt say to us? Have we ever tried something like this? That is, have we ever refrained from eating because no one was around—because we didn't want to eat without anyone? We've all probably waited at a restaurant because a friend was late and we waited to sit down until he arrived (or because the maître d'hôtel wouldn't seat us until our full party arrived). But how many of us have ever cooked dinner and then waited for someone to knock on the door or ring the doorbell when we didn't even send out an invite? Yeah, me neither. Because that would be weird. Why would we wait for someone to eat with us?

Putting Fasting and Feasting in Perspective

What is fasting? What is feasting? What does it look like to fast and to feast? Why are they important? Most of us understand the nature of feasting, so we don't need to spend too much time discussing it. Below we'll note the importance of practicing it. Fasting, however, is often misunderstood. Yet when we really think about it, we know it to be some form of abstention. To abstain from something is to willingly step away from it for a brief time and for a good reason. We voluntarily deny ourselves something that we want or something that we ordinarily consume or enjoy for some noteworthy reason. Most of us understand this, even though we wouldn't define fasting in this way. Some of us might also realize that typically after the allotted time is up and we've accomplished what we set out to do, we return to this thing that we ordinarily consume or enjoy. But this latter part isn't always clear to many.

Another practice like fasting that we typically confuse with the latter is abstemiousness. Abstemiousness is the practice of not being self-indulgent in food and drink. The root of the word is associated with drink more than food, but it applies to both. An abstemious person is someone who doesn't eat or drink too much. He is neither a glutton nor does he starve himself. When we typically talk about someone being abstemious, we don't mean that he's abstaining from food and drink; we mean that he's restrained in his consumption of food and drink. It's not that he isn't eating or drinking; he's doing it moderately and even meagerly. Unlike with fasting, he consistently and frequently eats.

We also confuse fasting with temperance, which is the more basic motivation and framework for abstemiousness. Temperance can be applied to many things and activities, but for our purposes, the temperate eater would be someone who doesn't abstain from eating excessively or deficiently time and again but rather all the time. He eats just the right amount. This sounds a lot like abstemiousness, and they are very similar because abstemiousness is a form of temperance. Yet they differ in one nuanced respect: abstemiousness avoids indulgence; temperance avoids excessiveness. It's one thing to not indulge and another to never overindulge. The temperate person is moderate in his lifestyle and not simply in an act here or there, as the abstemious person is with food and drink. As a lifestyle—with features that are hitched to the practice of simplicity—temperance goes beyond mere eating and drinking.

We have to be careful here: there are other practices we could also confuse with fasting, such as continence, forbearance, and abnegation. Continence is a form of self-restraint similar to temperance, but it usually refers to sexuality. It implies restraining one's sexual activity. Forbearance is self-restraint, but it involves a higher degree of struggle than other forms of self-restraint. Those who are abstemious or temperate want to be self-restrained in whatever they do, but they struggle to do so because deep down, they want to do otherwise. They tolerate practicing restraint. Fasting is not the same as forbearance because fasting is not merely tolerated. Finally, fasting is not abnegation. Those who abnegate something reject or renounce it. The thing is bad, and those who abnegate make it known as such. They stay away from it and warn people not to partake in it. Fasting, however, is not a rejection of food, but a refraining from partaking in it for a time.

At their most basic level, fasting and feasting are ways of eating. They are practices that get us to step away from food and step back to food. They prompt us to withdraw from food in our eating (fasting) and involve ourselves more in food and others (feasting) when we eat. As we will come to see, eating is more than stuffing our faces and making the growling in our stomachs go away. Similarly, fasting is more than not eating, and feasting is more than eating a great deal. Both practices foster and facilitate sharing, giving, and consuming food with others as we eat. In fasting, we don't reject food and starve ourselves but value food enough to abstain from it and give it to others. In feasting, we don't hoard our food and only enjoy it ourselves but celebrate with others and share our food. Both of these disciplines are about developing a right relationship to food and strengthening our relationship with our neighbor in and with and through our eating and nourishment.

Loving Our Neighbor with Our Tummies and Urges

Many of us brought up in the Christian tradition were likely taught that the spiritual discipline of fasting involves hearing from God, and feasting involves . . . well, actually, we've probably never heard about this one in church. We probably heard of it from non-Christians. We'll get to that. Fasting, as we were told or as we inferred from the lived practice of those around us, is about hearing from God. The laid-off husband fasts to discern what God has in store for him in the future. Or the sister fasts because she needs patience and kindness after just having a massive fight with her brother. Some of us may have even observed fasts around the liturgical calendar; during Lent, for example. For most of us, financial struggles, anxiety about an annual checkup at the doctor's office, guilt during the season of Lent, or a fund-raiser for the youth group give us reason to fast.

While these are legitimate concerns to bring to God, we've left out something important. We have missed some important reasons for fasting, not to mention some important ways to fast. Not only this, but we have also missed some important reasons for feasting as a regular practice. Fasting is about much more than simply listening to and hearing from God; and feasting is about much more than simply celebrating our achievements or blessings from God. We have overlooked something in the original design for both practices: their horizontal dimension. Fasting and feasting are more about our neighbor and her well-being and livelihood than whatever benefit we get from them. They are meant to benefit and bless her, not primarily or exclusively ourselves.

We see this clearly in the book of Isaiah. In the following passage God describes the kind of fast and feast that he chooses, which explains how and why we should fast and feast. And it's clear from the passage that we can and should discipline our eating habits and practices.

> "Why do we fast, but you do not see?
>   Why humble ourselves, but you do not notice?"
> Look, you serve your own interest on your fast day,
>   and oppress all your workers.
> Look, you fast only to quarrel and to fight
>   and to strike with a wicked fist.
> Such fasting as you do today
>   will not make your voice heard on high.

Is such the fast that I choose,
a day to humble oneself?
Is it to bow down the head like a bulrush,
and to lie in sackcloth and ashes?
Will you call this a fast,
a day acceptable to the LORD?

Is not this the fast that I choose:
to loose the bonds of injustice,
to undo the thongs of the yoke,
to let the oppressed go free,
and to break every yoke?
Is it not to share your bread with the hungry,
and bring the homeless poor into your house;
when you see the naked, to cover them,
and not to hide yourself from your own kin?

(Isa. 58:3–7)

The fast that God chooses, at least according to this passage in Isaiah, is one that loosens wickedness and liberates yokes of oppression on our neighbor. It's one that benefits our neighbor, not just us. God clearly cares about our neighbor and how our eating habits and practices impact her livelihood. "Share your bread with the hungry" (Isa. 58:7). "Offer your food to the hungry and satisfy the needs of the afflicted" (Isa. 58:10). These are admonitions to change how we eat, and they run contrary to any form of selfish eating, whether it is greedy monopolizing or miserly eating. God tells us that the proper ways to eat involve helping, not hurting, our neighbor.

The theme of "sharing your bread with the hungry" through the practice of fasting was common in the early church and in early monastic communities too. Gregory the Great, for example, says that "a man fasts not to God but to himself, if he does not give to the poor what he denies his belly for a time, but reserves it to be given to his belly later."[4] For Gregory, fasting is not about taking a short break from food in order to hear from God, only to go back to eating a few days later. It's about sharing food. It's about liberating others. It's about helping others with our resources and tummies. It's about sacrificing what we would eat so that we can give it to those in need.

Feasting serves a similar purpose and goes hand in hand with fasting. The word "feast" is tied to the Latin word for a "festival," *festum*. In fact, a feast is a festival—it's a well-organized, joyful celebration. It's well organized in the sense that you don't throw a feast together a few minutes beforehand. It's not an impromptu get-together. It's planned, and invitations are sent out. It's a joyful celebration in the sense that it's an important party thrown to commemorate a past event or achievement, although this isn't always the case. You don't have to wait to feast until you reach a milestone at work or birth a child. There are many things for which we could feast: life, health, our family, gainful employment, and so forth. And a feast always includes others—no one feasts alone. Of course, it always includes food. Lots and lots of food. And the best food that we can offer.

A feast involves others, and it involves inviting these others. In the Gospel of Luke (14:12–24), Jesus tells us about feasting. In particular, he instructs us as to whom we should invite when have a feast (or a banquet). His instructions are radical and somewhat unsettling.

> When you give a luncheon or a dinner, do not invite your friends or your brothers or your relatives or rich neighbors, in case they may invite you in return, and you would be repaid. But when you give a banquet, invite the poor, the crippled, the lame, and the blind. And you will be blessed, because they cannot repay you, for you will be repaid at the resurrection of the righteous. (vv. 12–14)

Jesus essentially tells us that when we throw a party or a banquet or a feast, we should invite only those in need. Don't invite those who already have wealth and possessions. Don't invite those who have food in their refrigerators and cupboards. Don't invite those who have money to repay you. Don't invite your family and friends. Invite the stranger. Invite those who don't have anything. Invite those who can't repay you. Put energy into throwing a party and use your time and resources to bless strangers and those in need.

These are radical and unsettling words, are they not? Throw a huge party but don't invite the people you love and the people who love you. Invite those who don't know you or those you don't know. Invite those you are supposed to love even though they are not friends from childhood or members of your family. These are words we need to hear, are they not? These are words of truth to the selfish eater. We don't want to share our best wine and viands with others, especially the needy. We don't want to share our goods with those who do not benefit us. We would rather give and share with those in whom we invest or those who will pay it forward—that is, back to us. But the parable about feasting in Luke and the passage about fasting in Isaiah tell us that our eating practices should in some way benefit those in need, not those whom we find beneficial or advantageous to ourselves.

A feast is about inviting our neighbor over to nourish herself and celebrate with us. We organize and host it, and we share our resources with her. We welcome her into our home or place of intimacy to dine with us—to sit at our table and to be served by us. Dining can be an intimate affair, and many of us are reluctant to dine with others because of that. It makes us vulnerable. Our manners (or lack thereof) are on the table, so to speak. And when it comes to celebrating with others, we are choosy. We don't act like ourselves around everyone, and at a celebration we host, we definitely want to be ourselves. A feast pushes back on these selfish and insecure tendencies. We share the best of our best with our neighbor (Judg.

6:19). We fellowship with her. We talk to her. We catch up with her. Maybe we get to know her for the first time.

At the heart of fasting and feasting is the idea that our time, our tables, and our tummies belong to God. Our natural urges belong to him. He is the Creator, Redeemer, and Restorer of our tummies. God calls us to steward these gifts in ways that lift up and love our neighbor and heal and harmonize our world. We are supposed to use our food and forks for his purposes, not for our own satisfaction and mere enjoyment. He invites us to share these things with those in need. He invites us to bless and benefit others with what he has given us and with the gifts we prize the most: the elements that sustain and nourish us.

If there's anything we know about Jesus, it's that he actively tried to bless and benefit others with his eating habits and practices. He ate in ways that demonstrated and facilitated love. He loved with and through his eating. On the one hand, he shared his food. He broke bread with others (Matt. 26:26), and he did so frequently. He multiplied what others had and provided even more for people (John 6:11). On the other hand, he ate with others. He helped and healed relationships by eating with those who didn't deserve to eat with him and whom others didn't want to associate with. Zacchaeus, for example, was a tax collector (Luke 19:1–10). Jesus knew that human eating was designed for more than satiated, individual bloated tummies.

In the routine of our daily nourishment and enjoyment, we frequently and easily eat selfishly. For example, we acquire our food mindlessly without consideration of our neighbor's need. We possess our food without sharing it or giving it to our neighbor. We even consume our food quickly and selfishly without enjoying it with our neighbor.[5] We could use a little discipline in our urges. We would do well to curb our tummies and control our eating habits and practices. We can do this through the disciplines of fasting and feasting.

Fasting and feasting are disciplines that remedy and renew our malformed ways of eating. When we fast and feast, we push back on our selfish and sinful eating. Fasting and feasting invite us not only to eat with our neighbor, which might be something we do every day, but also to share our food with our neighbor and give her the best that we have, which probably isn't something we do every day. When we fast, as described in Isaiah, our neighbor, not ourselves, becomes the recipient of our food. In feasting, as described in Luke, fellowship with our neighbor becomes the goal of our eating, not merely nourishment. Contemporary theologian Norman Wirzba states this well when he says, "People should feast so they do not forget the grace and the blessing of the world. People should fast so they do not degrade or hoard the good gifts of God."[6] Fasting and feasting are companion practices that serve the same purpose: correcting the way that we eat. But as we've seen, they reform our practices in different ways. Fasting corrects our greedy and dominative eating as we graft giving to our neighbor into everyday eating practices. Feasting corrects dominative and miserly eating as we graft sharing with our neighbor into everyday eating practices. Central to both disciplines is a concern for our neighbor's nourishment, well-being, and concrete social and economic conditions.

In a world where we cower in our cubicle for an hour in the middle of the day, eat takeout with our office door locked, and hear of people starving across the world or in our own backyards, the practices of fasting and feasting can be acts of love toward our neighbor. These practices discipline our urges and tummies so they begin to yearn for our neighbor's needs and for fellowship. Our neighbor then becomes an essential component of our nourishment and celebration of life. By feasting and fasting, we get into the habit of giving and sharing the most basic elements of our lives: food and drink. Fasting gets us to deny our tummies so we can donate what's on our table, and feasting gets us to celebrate with our neighbor and consume the best of the best in our cupboards.

If we are committed citizens of God's kingdom, we need to have our gustatory holes sanctified and our kitchens renewed to witness to our King's rule. If we're honest with ourselves, all of us need to tweak our eating tendencies and traditions to some degree. In the coming kingdom, sacrificing for our neighbor and sharing our resources will no longer be a nice thing to do; it will be the normal thing to do. In the meantime, we can love our neighbor in simple activities by making small adjustments to our eating habits and practices. We can love our neighbor in and through our daily deeds. By making the practices of fasting and feasting a rhythm of our day or week and by making slight changes to our current eating practices, we can contribute to our neighbor's well-being and make a positive contribution to her livelihood. Giving, sharing, and fellowshiping with our neighbor can contribute to her wants and needs.

Side Steps: Fasting and Feasting

Prayer

Father, Giver of life, you nourish and sustain us through the simplest of elements. The gifts you give us from the ground and the sky give us power and energy to bring forth new gifts from you, such as our daily deeds for our neighbor. Thanks be to you. Through your son, Jesus Christ, teach us to use this energy and power to help and heal those who need it. Inspire and empower us to share our food and resources as Jesus did. Help make our few loaves, or our crumbs even, bring life to the world. Holy Spirit, guide us and grant us wisdom in how we give and share. Lead us to give and share despite a lack of supply. Comfort us in our sacrifice, and give us courage to give even when we are in need. All for your name's sake and our neighbor's security. Amen.

Simple Steps to Practice Fasting and Feasting

- When fasting, let conscience and liberty be your guide. Take into account time, manner, quality, conditions, age, and so forth. Be sensitive to your abilities and limits. If you have a medical condition and can't fast for an entire day, fast for one meal or forgo an afternoon snack. Remember: consistency and regularity are the most important. Do what you can. But make sure to give what you don't eat to someone in need!

- At work, try buying lunch for someone soliciting or begging for change outside your building. If you're free at home, take a nice meal to the homeless shelter, a new mom in the hospital, or a resident at a senior living community. Or buy groceries for college students so they're not eating ramen noodles for months. Look around you and find someone in need.

- Do you have something to celebrate? A work promotion? Your child's birthday? The anniversary of buying your home? Celebrate it with others. Invite over friends, family, and neighbors. Crack open that really expensive bottle of wine and cook that perfect steak. Share the gifts God has given you with others while they share in the gifts God has given you.

+ + + + + + + + +

FIVE

+ + + + + + + + +

TIME-OUT FOR ADULTS

SOLITUDE AND RENEWED SOCIALIZING

"She left! She left!" I thought to myself. "I can't believe it."

It was the first major fight I ever had with my wife (at the time girlfriend). We had been dating for only a few months. It was a Friday evening, and we had just finished watching a movie—I think Tom Cruise was in it—in the basement of her dorm. I was still wearing my basketball gear from an earlier practice and held an empty blue Gatorade bottle in my hand. "What are we doing tomorrow?" These were the words that started it all.

What happened next is a bit fuzzy, but before the Gatorade bottle hit the poster, the trifecta of poor decision making (i.e., regret, guilt, and shame) had slid through my veins and collided with my heart. My tongue was dry. My biceps and fingers were tingly. My back was painfully stout. It was incredulity that kept me standing there for at least a minute. I was incapacitated. "What just happened?" I thought to myself. Truth be told, it all seemed a bit impulsive. I turned around and saw the face of blankness, only to see it turn around and walk away. Incredulity still had me by the collar. Eventually (another a minute later), I wiggled free and stormed after her. I looked up the stairwell. Nothing but glass and dust. She was gone.

I was raised in a home where you don't let the sun go down when you're angry (Eph. 4:26). You reconcile before you retire for the evening. Even though the sun was already down when I got angry this day, the principle still applied. I called her, and we talked for a while. Both of us were clear about expectations. "Okay, but don't walk out on me like that, please," I said sternly. "Okay, but I just needed a moment to think and breathe," she said. "I just needed a moment to gather my thoughts. . . . You were acting kind of crazy."

Socializing is basic to being human and to functioning as a human being. We hang out, stand alongside, and interact with people every day. Like all things human, socializing is done in community and with a community. Many of us can, at times, be alone, but we are also parents and lovers, siblings and children, friends and strangers, colleagues and citizens. We can't get away from ties to our community, and we interact and socialize with many communities on several levels. We rub shoulders with coworkers, we live next to family members, and we walk alongside strangers on the street. How and when we socialize and interact with others is informed by these others, and how and when we socialize and interact with others informs the wants and needs of others.

If we take an honest, close look at our socializing practices, many of us will agree that at times our socializing practices tend to be selfish and self-centered. We can hurt our neighbor with our absence or with our presence. Two selfish tendencies are worth noting: intrusion and avoidance. Both of these, to some degree, hurt our neighbor and negatively impact her livelihood. Although these might seem minor and therefore harmless things, selfish socializing can hurt our neighbor and negatively impact life in community with her.

Malformed Socializing: Intrusion

When Hank Palmer, in the film *The Judge* (2014), is informed that his mother has died, he catches a flight to his godforsaken hometown. After the funeral, he has a frustrating interaction with his father, Joseph Palmer, who is an Indiana judge (played by Robert Duvall). Hank later receives a phone call and learns that his father is being questioned by the local police about a fatal hit-and-run. Shortly thereafter his father is indicted.

Hank (played by Robert Downey Jr.) is an aggressive and arrogant defense lawyer who has never lost a case. Never. Hence the arrogance. When Joseph is indicted, he hires another defense attorney— not his son, Hank. Of course this decision frustrates Hank, and from day one he inserts himself into the case. He mocks the other attorney, shouts in court, and even derides his father. Eventually, the other attorney quits, and Hank's father "hires" Hank as his attorney.

Before Hank becomes his father's defense lawyer, his father doesn't want Hank to instruct the other attorney. He doesn't want Hank's advice on any legal matters. He doesn't even want him involved in the ordeal. Nevertheless, Hank intrudes. He imposes himself on his father's attorney. He inserts himself into his father's case. Sometimes his father is amused by this behavior, but for the most part he's troubled and frustrated by it. It causes tension in their already splintered relationship.

There will be times when we annoy and inconvenience our neighbor. We'll be around too much, or we won't be there enough. This happens with humans living in community or in close proximity to one another. We cross some kind of line, but we work it out. We make mistakes, but we ask for forgiveness and reconcile. We adjust to one another. We become clear about expectations. The memories of past annoyances and inconveniences begin to fade away, and the prospect of future annoyances decreases. We move on and try to live harmoniously with one another. This situation, however, is much different from consistently and frequently intruding on our neighbor and her way of life, which is what Hank did. Hank forced himself into situations and circumstances when and where he wasn't welcome. He was too present to his neighbors, which resulted in conflict and even a few irreparable relationships.

It may come as a shock to some of you, as it did for me, but there are times when we are not needed. There are times when our neighbor doesn't need our help. Your girlfriend doesn't need you to do it for her. Your employee can handle it himself. Your child can make up her own mind. Your friend doesn't need your advice. Your student doesn't need your counsel. When we disregard this and force ourselves into these situations anyway, we intrude and impose. Intrusion can take many forms. The most common one is to impose ourselves on our neighbor because we think our neighbor could use our help. This is what Hank did. We force ourselves on our neighbor and into her life even when unsolicited. We put ourselves in a place where we are not welcome. We try to control a situation that our neighbor hasn't invited us to help control. Adult children do it with elderly parents. Parents do it with teenagers. Distant aunts and uncles do it at funerals.

Intrusion is a malformed way to socialize. It is not the way that we see Jesus being present, that's for sure, and it is not the way Jesus calls us to interact. Intruding on others is a selfish way to socialize. We can and should love our neighbor with our presence and shadow, but we are not doing so when we intrude in her affairs. It's possible for us to be too present with her and for our shadow to overcast our neighbor and overwhelm her or drown her out. Consistent and frequent intrusion disrupts harmony with our neighbor and creates tense strains in our relationship with her. We may believe that our advice, financial assistance, or company is helpful to her, and maybe even necessary, but if she doesn't think so, then we need to be careful. When we force our presence on her, she may be offended or angered in a manner that makes it difficult for us to help her in the future.

Malformed Socializing: Avoiding Others

Set in the 1950s, the television show *Grantchester* stars an Anglican vicar named Sidney Chambers who ends up collaborating with a detective inspector in the village. Sidney is a borderline alcoholic priest-investigator who begins mentoring a curate, Leonard Finch. In season one, Leonard is about to skip town because he doesn't feel prepared for the priesthood. In his first sermon at his new parish, he mentioned the German philosopher Immanuel Kant, which led everybody and their mother to tune out. Leonard is sullen. Sidney meets Leonard and sits down with him. After a few remarks back and forth, Leonard says something that will probably resonate with most of us (especially those of us who have a nerdy side): "I like books. They're so much less terrifying than people." People indeed can be terrifying, can't they? Especially when there is conflict in a relationship. And sometimes you just want to get away altogether.

Most of us don't enjoy dealing with conflict or awkwardness. The easiest thing for us to do is just to get away from our neighbor. We've all avoided our neighbor at some point in our lives. She could be our neighbor next door or a patron at the coffee shop we frequent. We walk down a different street to avoid passing by her on our usual stroll. Or we check out other roasters in town for a few months. Or we settle for using the French press at home. The breakup could have gone very badly and things took a turn for the worse, so we choose the extreme route: we change churches or transfer schools. Why do we do such things? There are as many reasons why we avoid our neighbor as we have neighbors. "He's too loquacious." "She laughs really loudly." "He's intimidating." "I'm afraid I won't be able to hold

a conversation with him—he's got a PhD in chemistry!" "He smells."
"She's mean." "He's too serious and uptight about his faith." "I just
don't have time to hang out with her." "He drinks too much." "We
just don't like the same sorts of things." "She's not a Christian."

Like intrusion, avoiding others is not a true representation or
stewarding of our God-given ability to socialize—but a malformed
way to do it. Although there were times when Jesus needed space
(Mark 6:31), avoiding others was not the way he interacted with his
neighbor. Nor is it the way that Jesus calls us to interact with our
neighbors. How can we preach the gospel to someone or make her
a disciple if we avoid her? Like intrusion, avoiding others is a selfish
way to socialize. We can love our neighbor with our presence and
shadow, but we are not doing so when we avoid her. When we make
it a habit of avoiding our neighbor, and our neighbor notices it, we
damage our relationship with her. We disrupt communion with her.
Avoiding her causes the bond between us to unwind. We become
disconnected. We distrust each other. Slowly we become strangers.
Eventually opportunities to love her become scarce.

Solitude and Renewed Socializing

"Now, Elliott has had to 'take a break' a few times recently because
she was aggressive and bossy with [insert name of some unruly boy
who shouldn't be matriculating at her school]," the lead teacher said.

You can imagine my response when I heard these words a number
of years ago from the lead preschool teacher, as my wife and I sat
in kiddie chairs across from her and her "helper." We had recently
relocated from the Los Angeles area and enrolled our daughter
Elliott (age eight) in a private kindergarten through eighth-grade
school a few blocks from where we live. This was our first parent-
teacher conference, which was held about midway through the
fall semester.

Now, I didn't say "Huh?" but I thought it. Apparently I thought it so fiercely in my brain that the reverberations burst forth from my forehead and eyes so that the lead teacher could feel them. Despite my concern, she continued. After both she and her helper had finished giving us the lowdown on Elliott's progress in school, I went back to that "huh" and addressed the elephant in the room.

"So, she's been to time-out?"

"Well, yes. But we don't call it 'time-out,'" her teacher replied.

I was skeptical about what was coming next. But then something magical happened. She explained their practice of "taking a break" to my wife and me, and I'm not kidding when I say that my life will never be the same.

"Here at [insert name of the awesome school my daughter attends] we don't treat time-out like punishment," she said. "We encourage the kids to take a break when they feel frustrated or when others see that they are breaking our classroom covenant." (I later learned that there are five rules to the classroom covenant. The first two are "love one another" and "treat each other the way you want to be treated.") Elliot's teacher continued, "We tell them that it's a space for them to take a deep breath and come back when they're ready."

Walking home that evening I thought to myself, "How great would it be if adults were to take breaks like these kids do?" How different would the world be if we were to do something like this on a regular basis? What if we took some time every day to step away from community and our "playtime" together to evaluate our thoughts, attitudes, feelings, behavior, and lifestyle? What if we did this on our own initiative? What if others invited us to do this? What kind of people would we become if we stepped away from community at heated moments? Even better, what if we did this long before these heated moments? What if we incorporated a rhythm of time-out into our daily routine that could lead us to defuse and decrease these heated moments? What kind of colleagues and citizens would we become? How would that change our neighborhoods and cities?

Putting Solitude in Perspective

Jesus took breaks. He stepped away from community to evaluate his life. The Gospel of Mark opens with a passage telling us that "in the morning, while it was still very dark, [Jesus] got up and went out to a deserted place, and there he prayed" (Mark 1:35). What exactly is Jesus doing here? Many of us might assume or infer from this passage that Jesus is practicing solitude. He is going somewhere where no other human beings are around, and he's praying. But I wonder if this really is practicing solitude. Is solitude merely being alone? Does the frequent getting away from others count as practicing solitude? Is that all it takes? Must it include prayer? If it doesn't include prayer, then what is it? Does it cease being solitude? Does it cease being the practice of solitude? What exactly is solitude?

Like the other disciplines mentioned, solitude is often confused with other practices in society. In particular, it's often confused with other forms of withdrawal from community, one example being seclusion. Seclusion isn't merely withdrawing from community but involves shutting oneself off from community. For example, the mad scientist who spends years in his dungeon or condemned factory experimenting and making savage creatures has secluded himself. In order to engage in activities that would probably be ridiculed, condemned, or misunderstood by human society, the mad scientist has shut himself off and isolated himself from human contact. A prisoner in solitary confinement would be another, quite different example of seclusion, but his seclusion is forced on him and not voluntarily embraced.

Another form of withdrawal from human society often associated with solitude is vacation. This might seem a little strange, but we really do confuse the two. Vacation is when we step away from the hustle and bustle of work or family life to escape from our problems for a while. Some of us run off to a tropical island, while others spend a week at an overcrowded water park. Some may visit family on the shore or ensconce themselves in their "man cave" for a few days. Wherever we may go to vacate, we take this time to escape our tasks and responsibilities for a while. We go somewhere to be idle and lazy, so we can chill. But then, after this brief time is up, we grudgingly return to the tasks and responsibilities that we escaped for a week or two—supposedly rejuvenated—to face society once again.

Solitude is neither of these two forms of withdrawal. It is neither a temporary suspension from life in community nor an escape. The word "solitude" means "alone" (from the Latin *solus*). But being alone, as we will see in a second, does not translate to secluding oneself or isolating oneself from human contact. It doesn't mean intentionally shutting oneself off from others. Yet this misconception continues to hold sway in contemporary culture. As one writer recently put it: "Solitude is ultimately an illusion, a fantasy that can be enjoyed for a while but must always end in acknowledging others—how they make us who we are, in the world we share with our dolls and tigers and all the ghosts of past, present and yet to come."[1] Solitude, however, is not a shutting off from others but a stepping away from society.

Just because we find ourselves lacking contact with another human being doesn't mean that we're alone. If we find ourselves in some distant place alone, or we get away for a short while once a year, this hardly means that we're practicing solitude. Practicing solitude means that we're deliberate about stepping away from community repeatedly and regularly. The one who practices solitude steps away from society but then returns shortly thereafter. He steps away for a brief time, not an indefinite period. And he steps away from society not to escape from his tasks and responsibilities but, as we will see, out of concern for them. He gets away not to be idle or lazy but to be occupied in a different way. Practicing solitude is about rightly relating to our neighbor. It's about getting into a healthy rhythm of socializing so that we can dwell and commune more harmoniously.

Loving Our Neighbor with Our Shadow and Presence

If we truly want to love our neighbor as ourselves, then we need to change how we interact with her. We need to change how often we interact with her. Some of us need to stop avoiding her and start interacting with her. Most of us probably need to give her space and take time to reflect and pray about the needs and demands of our life together. We cannot love our neighbor if we avoid her and are absent from her life. Similarly, we cannot love her if our presence is constantly disruptive or domineering in her life. We could probably do a better job of loving her with our shadow and presence. One small but significant way we can do this is by altering our daily deeds and our everyday socializing so that we can take breaks. Consistently and frequently stepping away from our neighbor to think and pray and stepping once again toward her to refresh community and possibly deal with any issues in our life together will help us love her on a much deeper level and in other activities we do.

Those of us brought up in the Christian tradition were probably taught that the spiritual discipline of solitude has to do with getting away from the world so we can listen to God. It allows us to drop all our concerns in life and focus on God. It gives us a time to get rejuvenated and refreshed from laboring in our worldly affairs. Jesus is often our point of reference for this. Apparently he practiced solitude (Luke 5:16), and apparently he did this by going into the wilderness or to a deserted place (Matt. 4:1–2; Mark 1:12–13; Luke

5:15–16), ascending a mountain (Luke 6:12–13), taking a boat out on a lake (Matt. 14:13), or walking through a garden (Matt. 26:36). He seemed to step away from the world to be alone with God. Apparently Jesus needed some time to foster intimacy with God in order to continue his ministry.

Of course, occasionally stepping away from our tasks and responsibilities to talk to and hear from God is something we must do. We are often busy, and our lives are noisy. We need to take time to reflect, pray, and listen. Be that as it may, this understanding of solitude reduces its meaning. Solitude is much bigger than this. When we're so focused on what this practice does for us, we risk missing something important about practicing this discipline. "Being alone with God"—is that all there is to solitude? Jesus didn't go away just to be with God, did he? That's not the only reason he stepped away, is it? There's more to be gained from this practice than merely alone time with God. There's a horizontal dimension to this practice that merits consideration.

Why did Jesus step away to pray? What was he praying for? Why did he withdraw at the moment(s) that he did? To get in touch with the Father and to get the strength he needed to endure his work? Perhaps. But was it only about Jesus and the Father? Might Jesus have done it for others? Perhaps for his disciples? While he was away from them, could he have been praying for them? Could a conversation with them have prompted his stepping away? Was he praying for the future of the church? Was he praying for his present situation? What was he thinking about during this time? What was he doing? Why, exactly, was he doing this?

If we read closely, between the lines, we can see that at times Jesus withdrew from society because circumstances were tense. His interaction with others in his community wasn't going the way it should. Did Jesus get frustrated with Peter sometimes (John 21:15–19)? Did he get angry with people now and again (Mark 3:5)?

Was he occasionally put off by John or James (Mark 10:35–40)? Were others in community with him at times selfish and self-centered? Yes. Definitely. On one occasion, people wanted to forcibly make him king (John 6:15), which, as we know, wasn't his plan. Another time some people started to mooch or scrounge off him, and he wasn't having it (John 6:26). What did Jesus do? He stepped away from community and returned later. He walked away for a time; he took away his shadow and presence for the health of communing with others.

Several times like these (and perhaps many more not recorded in the Bible) Jesus withdrew from others—not only because he needed to hear from the Father or be rejuvenated by the Spirit—but because his relationship with others had become unhealthy or harmful. His interaction and socializing with others wasn't right. Even though he is the light of the world, Jesus was aware of how his presence might cast too much of a shadow on his followers. Of course, the blame rested on those interacting and socializing with Jesus. Perhaps in these moments Jesus felt that these people were imposing on him. At the very least, as we see in John 6:15, they were trying to impose their own agenda on him. Conversely, many times Jesus approached those who were probably avoiding him—Jews, prostitutes, Pharisees, and even his own disciples. In these instances, it seems that Jesus stepped away from others or stepped toward them out of concern for life together. He practiced solitude out of concern for the community.

At the heart of solitude is the idea that we live in and were made for community. We cannot truly escape community: we have ecological inheritances from family, friends, and strangers before us who planted and tilled; biological ties to family who birthed, raised, and supported us; the social influence of family, friends, and strangers who educated and cultured us; and the political responsibilities for which we are implicitly accountable. Community is a huge part of our lives, and it's important that we care for and give back to community. This is how God made the world. And it is to community that we are called. Our presence and shadows belong to God. Our attendance and participation are his. He calls us to use our presence and shadows to lift up and love our neighbor and to heal and harmonize our world.

Henry David Thoreau, an American essayist and poet, is famously known for his two-year experiment during which he built a tiny cabin near Walden Pond, outside Concord, Massachusetts, for just under thirty dollars. It was an experiment in self-sufficiency: Thoreau wanted to know what he really needed to live. He provides an account of this in *Walden; Or, Life in the Woods* (1854), in which he reflects on solitude. At the end of the chapter on solitude, Thoreau says the following:

> Society is commonly too cheap. We meet at very short intervals, not having had time to acquire any new value for each other. We meet at meals three times a day, and give each other a new taste of that old musty cheese that we are. We have had to agree on a certain set of rules, called etiquette and politeness, to make this frequent meeting tolerable and that we need not come to open war. We meet at the post-office, and at the sociable, and about the fireside every night; we live thick and are in each other's way, and stumble over one another, and I think that we thus lose some respect for one another. Certainly less frequency would suffice for all important and hearty communications. . . . It would be better if there were but one inhabitant to a square mile, as where I live.[2]

Thoreau tended to conflate solitude with isolation. But here he clearly understands that it's possible for us to be too present to one another. In the hustle and bustle of our daily lives, our presence and shadows can easily become agents of harm in our communities. We can lose control of our presence in community and not be aware of how we are interacting within that community. We lose sight of how we affect our neighbor. And we don't often take time to assess how our neighbor feels about our presence. Our presence can become overbearing, and a fleeing or overcasting shadow can disrupt our neighbor. Too much of us and too little of us can hurt her. Our impositions and avoidances can, if not checked, destroy communion with our neighbor. Thoreau, and more importantly Jesus, was clued into these malformed ways that we socialize and interact with our neighbor.

We could use some discipline for our presence. We need to box with our shadow a little bit and shape it to care for our neighbor. We need to check how frequently and vastly we are present with our neighbor. Are we around enough or too much? Do we meddle? Are we indifferent or do we interfere? We need to control our patterns of social interaction. We need a way to become more aware of others and pay attention to their well-being as we are in relationship with them. As Thoreau suggests and Jesus demonstrated, practicing solitude is a helpful way to counteract these selfish ways of interacting with our neighbor.

Some of us go on yearlong sabbaticals or attend weekend church retreats at a monastery a few hours away. We go away for a time to get ourselves right. We might even fast and meditate during this time. These practices are great, but they don't really get to the heart of the matter. At the end of the day, they don't really change our life together with our neighbor. How are we interacting with our neighbor for the six years before we take our sabbatical? How do we treat our neighbor before we go on that weekend church retreat? We take an occasional break to lift our spirits, but for the rest of the year our presence runs amok and we ominously impose on others as if it's not a big deal. We're not aware of our socializing habits and patterns. We don't challenge how we tend to dwell in and inhabit spaces with others. We only discipline our presence and shadow annually or seasonally. We dabble in solitude; we don't practice it.

Solitude is a *practice* that remedies and renews our selfish socializing. When we practice solitude, we scale back our intrusive interactions with others. Out of concern for our impositions on others, we impose on ourselves a time-out or break. We give our neighbor space and time away from us. We step out of community; then at some point, we return, and if there has been a problem, we address the issue. If not, we come back welcomed and renewed. As Thoreau notes, time away from one another will not pull community apart but build it up. It will breathe vitality into conversations that are being suffocated or snuffed out. It will give us time and energy to reevaluate our neighbor's significance and inspire change in our behavior toward our neighbor. It might even lead us to respect her a little more, as Thoreau said. Because solitude is a deliberate stepping back from community, it simultaneously remedies intrusion and avoidance.

In a world of micromanaging supervisors and online stalkers, overpopulation and workaholism, private mansions and acred ranches, daily breaks or time-outs from various communities and society at large would be acts of love toward our neighbor. These breaks, taken as we practice solitude, lead us to discipline our presence and shadow frequently and consistently. We get into the habit of checking our overbearing presence or our tendency to flee and giving ourselves (and our neighbor) time to evaluate our life together in community on an interpersonal level. This solitude can be a time for us to ask questions: How have others been perceiving me lately? Are they easily annoyed with me? Are they terse with me? What has my attitude been toward them? Have I been distant? What do others expect of me? What sorts of initiatives and responses do they expect from me? How and where could I exemplify Jesus to them?

An important way to love our neighbor on an interpersonal level and in the little things is to find a healthy balance between being absent and ever present, avoiding her and intruding on her affairs. In a world of broken promises, absentee fathers, and transient friends, being present to her in a time of need or letting her know that we are there for her is an act of love. But in a world of seven billion people, intentionally giving her space is also an act of love. When we are intrusive, we try to make our neighbor like us. When we avoid her, we indirectly try to make her no longer *our* neighbor. A step in truly loving her is not walking away from her or making her into our image but giving her space to be herself, a neighbor.[3] We can do this in small increments: fifteen minutes here or an hour there. We can do this during lunch break or before picking the kids up from school. We don't have to backpack through Europe or drive two hours away to a monastery. All we have to do is alter our schedule a little bit and be more aware of and intentional about our neighbor's needs.

An analogy with online media bears mentioning here.[4] We don't have community only among physical persons; we have it with digital avatars and profiles. In our day and age, flesh and bone do not need to be bumping into each other in order for community to exist. Life together is also online. We are close to and connected with these "people," and we interact and socialize with them too. It's important to recognize this and to acknowledge that many of us are members of online communities that are not in our city or our town. We need to discipline our digital presence and shadow on our devices, too. We also need to develop a healthy rhythm of solitude and socializing online. We need to take breaks from social media—Snapchat, Instagram, Twitter, Facebook, and email. Not to get away from it, of course, before it consumes us, as baby boomers and some Gen Xers are wont to say, but, rather, to take a break from it so that we can remedy and renew our "streaming" life together.

Side Steps: Solitude

Prayer

Heavenly Father, you created us in your image to commune with you. You then saw that it was not good for us to be alone so you threw us even further into community. Yet daily we turn from community by avoiding others. Daily we disrupt community by imposing ourselves on others. God, forgive us for making our lives about us. Forgive us for unraveling the community we share in you. Jesus, teach us how to reach out to those whom we think are unworthy, different, rebellious, and insignificant. Spirit, in moments of frustration, anger, insecurity, anxiety, and indifference, help us to gather ourselves and gravitate toward our neighbor in healing and reconciliation. For your glory and our witness we pray. Amen.

Simple Steps to Practice Solitude

- Remember that practicing solitude is about daily deeds. It's about consistency and frequency. Don't try to take time to be alone three days a month. Instead, carve out fifteen minutes a day. At work, if you sense tension and feel that you may have annoyed people in the morning, go for a walk on your lunch break. At home, after putting the kids to bed, leave your spouse in charge and go for a short walk.

- Don't underestimate the value of "taking a break" in the bathroom. The restroom is a great space to step away from the crowd and talk to God. Don't read that magazine or check your phone. Just sit there and think about how you're doing life together with others. Pray.

- Getting angry at the kids? Frustrated with the spouse or the roomies? If the washer and dryer are in the basement or garage or down the street, go do laundry. Take a little trip to the grocery store and pick up something you need. Calm yourself. Talk to God. Think about the kids, spouse, or roomies and how to be more patient, kind, and loving toward them.

- Here are some questions I ask myself during my time-outs. Maybe they will be helpful for you during your time.

  » Have I thought ill of anyone today?

  » How did I treat [insert name of student, colleague, spouse, lover, child, or some other type of neighbor] today?

  » Did I miss an opportunity to help anyone?

  » Did I take something that I didn't need and another could have used?

  » Did I share something with someone today? If not, what could I have shared?

  » Were my words kind and said in a loving way?

  » What do I do that annoys, frustrates, or hurts [insert name of student, colleague, spouse, lover, child, or some other type of neighbor]? How could I do things differently?

SIX

CONTROLLING THE CHATTERBOX

SILENCE AND RENEWED TALKING

If you're familiar with the children's book series Mr. Men and Little Miss, authored by Roger Hargreaves, then you've probably come across *Little Miss Chatterbox*. I didn't have the privilege of reading these books growing up, and I didn't even know that they existed until my daughter got one for her birthday. Both series contain fascinating characters that, I think, can get our kids talking about virtuous and vicious character traits and the importance of being sensitive to our neighbor's needs, expectations, and wishes.

Little Miss Chatterbox begins like this:

> Little Miss Chatterbox talked more than a lot.
> She talked all the time.
> Day in and day out, week after week, month after month,
>   year in and year out.
> She never stopped!
> She didn't know it, but she even talked in her sleep!

> She had a brother.
> I bet you can guess what his name was!
> Can't you?
> That's right!
> Mr. Chatterbox!
>
> . . . .
>
> You should have heard them when they got together!
> You couldn't get a word in edgeways.
> Or sideways.
> Or anyways![1]

If you've read the book or know anything about Miss Chatterbox's story, you know that her incessant chattering gets her into constant trouble. In fact, her jibber-jabbering concretely impacts her situation in some pretty significant ways: it gets her fired from several jobs and annoys quite a few friends and customers in the process. She's not mean, though—she doesn't chew anyone out or anything like that. She isn't terse with people. She isn't rude. Her curse is that she has a motormouth, and apparently no one likes it.

Like all the activities we've discussed in previous chapters, talking is basic to being human and functioning as a human being. We talk and communicate in some capacity every day. And like the other activities we've mentioned, this, too, is a privilege done in community and with the help of community. Parents, teachers, strangers, enemies, and lovers teach us how to speak. Someone drilled us with grammar exercises. Many people contributed to our vocabulary bank. Many, many people taught us the languages we know, the slang we use, and the gestures we make. Our speech derives from a community, and it is a community that understands our manner and style of talking and what it means. In turn, the community's manner and style of talking are informed by ours.

If we take an honest, close look at our talking habits and practices, many of us will see that they, as with the other activities we've discussed, tend to be selfish and self-centered. Like Miss Chatterbox, we utter too many words or we say the wrong words. We can hurt our neighbor with our tongue and words. I want to single out two selfish tendencies in the talking habits and practices of our North American democratic culture that I think, to some degree, hurt our neighbor and negatively impact our life together with her. A mean word here or the lack of an encouraging word there may seem insignificant and silly. But if we are not careful, it can hurt others inhabiting shared space with us and the life together we have with them.

Malformed Talking: Talkativeness

One way that we tend to be selfish in our talking is by being too talkative. One of my favorite characters on *Saturday Night Live* is Target Lady (played by Kristen Wiig). Target Lady is an over-enthusiastic, slightly dense, and disturbingly cheerful cashier who consistently accosts her customers with a boisterous greeting: "Hi, welcome to Target!" She startles, shocks, and scares customer after customer with this greeting and her enthusiasm and cheer. More than that, she talks to herself. She mumbles. She rarely "hears" the customers and what they have to say. As soon as they say something that piques her interest, she interrupts them or does something quirky to set them off. When customers get the chance to respond to something she says, she quickly responds in return. Sometimes she randomly runs to buy merchandise that her customers are purchasing, leaving them to wait for her to return before they can check out.

Many things are wrong with Target Lady's interaction with customers. Most customers become frustrated with her. Some just leave the store without their merchandise. Very few seem to enjoy her talkativeness and excessive cheerfulness. She's like a human Miss

Chatterbox—except for the fact that she's not real either. But if anything, it's her talkativeness that frustrates customers the most. They just want to purchase their merchandise and get out of there, but she wants to chitchat. For those occasional customers who don't mind talking, they too eventually get frustrated because she talks way too much and doesn't let them get a word in edgewise. They cannot talk to her because she's always talking to them. Her voice and words dominate their time together and commandeer the interaction between the two of them. As the viewer sees time and time again, it's off-putting, frustrating, and hurtful.

Talkativeness or loquaciousness can run in different directions. On the one hand is garrulity. Garrulity is a kind of loquaciousness, but it goes beyond simple talkativeness to chitchatting about unimportant things. Someone who is talkative can be talking about really important stuff, but people who are garrulous talk too much about trivial things. They chatter. They prattle. They talk about inconsequential things. On the other hand is verbosity, which is another kind of loquaciousness. Verbosity is the use of too many words. It doesn't necessarily mean one is chatty though. The verbose person could simply be someone who uses too many words to explain something simple. They could say it in a much more concise way, but they embellish or "beat around the bush" so to speak.

Talking too much may seem like a silly and trivial matter, but as we see from examples such as Target Lady and Miss Chatterbox (or consider Will Ferrell's character from *Elf*) and especially our experiences of people in our own lives, drowning others out by talking too much can be a hurtful and damaging enterprise. We don't like being drowned out. We don't like being unable to get a word in edgewise. We don't like being ignored. We don't enjoy being interrupted. We consistently find chatterboxes annoying. Very few of us are able to get used to them. As we all know, if we don't feel heard, we begin to feel slighted, ignored, and unappreciated. Not to mention, as some of us know from lived experience and our own mistakes, talkativeness can lead to "verbal vices," as they were called in medieval times, such as quarreling, spreading rumors, and boasting. Too much talking can get us talking about things that we shouldn't.

Talkativeness or loquaciousness is not a type of talking but a malformed way to talk. We don't know exactly how often Jesus spoke, but talkativeness doesn't seem consistent with his character (Matt. 12:19; 26:63). It's not how he used his words, and it doesn't seem to be the way that Jesus commissions us to use our words. It's a selfish way to talk. We can and should love our neighbor with our tongues and words, but we are not doing so when we talk excessively and drown her out. Too many words thrown at her, even if done with good intention, can push our neighbor away from us and negatively impact our communion with her. (Conversely, taciturnity, or saying little, could also be an issue in our lived interaction with our neighbor.) It doesn't really matter if our words are uplifting or edifying; too much talking and not enough listening can damage our life together with others.

Malformed Talking: Maligning Others

Another way that we tend to be selfish in our talking is by maligning others.

Miranda Priestly (played by Meryl Streep) in *The Devil Wears Prada* (2006) is the epitome of someone who maligns others. A snooty fashion magazine editor, Miranda not only critiques her subordinates, but she also attacks them and speaks evilly of them. She does this to their faces as well as behind their backs. For example, after one of her subordinates makes a mistake, albeit a major one, she says,

> Do you know why I hired you? I always hire the same girl—stylish, slender, of course . . . worships the magazine. But so often, they turn

out to be—I don't know—disappointing and, um . . . stupid. So you,
with that impressive résumé and the big speech about your so-called
work ethic—I, um—I thought you would be different. I said to myself, go ahead. Take a chance. Hire the smart, fat girl. I had hope.
My God. I live on it. Anyway, you ended up disappointing me more
than, um—more than any of the other silly girls.

Viewers of the film, unsettled, sit back and watch Miranda's subordinates become disturbed, upset, frustrated, wounded, and even
devastated by words like these. Miranda not only negatively impacts
her relationship with her neighbors; she unravels community at
home, at work, and on the street.

Malignity is evil speech. It is to "throw shade" on our neighbor. It
is to deliberately hurt her with our words. The word "malign" might
seem a little strong. But anytime we intentionally try to hurt our
neighbor with our words and do not build her up, we are maligning
her. We disrespect her. We ridicule her. We humiliate her. These
cannot be ways of building her up. To malign someone is very different from speaking critically of that person, though. Remember
from the last chapter that *mal* means bad. While we shouldn't speak
critically behind anyone's back, speaking critically of our neighbor,
if done correctly, can better her. It can build her up and spur her on
to better things. (All the art, food, and film critics can now breathe.)
But when we malign our neighbor, we don't say things that help
her improve; we say things to tear her down. We don't analyze; we
annihilate. We don't stop at evaluating; we excoriate.

Sometimes, of course, hurtful words can be said unintentionally.
We don't realize the weight of what we're saying, or we didn't know
that those particular words would wound our neighbor. When it
does happen, we apologize, reconcile, and move on. This is an accident, not a deliberate attempt to hurt our neighbor, which is what
we do when we malign her. Like talkativeness or loquacity, malignity

typically results in several other verbal vices, such as lying, insulting, mocking, or spreading rumors. And there seems to be a direct correlation between malignant speech and malicious thought. When we think and entertain malicious thoughts about our neighbor, malignant words easily flow from our lips. For us to malign our neighbor, some malicious thinking must be going on beforehand. The two are always found hand in hand.

Tearing someone down isn't going to be received well. When we say hurtful things about our neighbor to her face or behind her back, she's not going to like it. Malignant speech is not a type of talking but a malformed way to talk. It is not the way Jesus talked (Luke 4:22), and it is not the way that Jesus commands us to talk. Like talkativeness, malignant speech is a selfish way to talk. We can love our neighbor with and through our words, but we are not doing so when we speak ill of her. We cannot love our neighbor when we tear her down. We hurt our neighbor when we throw too many words at her, and we hurt her when we toss her the wrong words. We hurt her with "Blah, blah, blah, blah" (talkativeness), and we hurt her with "You're an idiot and no one likes you" (malignity). This kind of talk can push our neighbor away from us and negatively impact our communion with her.

Silence and the Renewal of Talking

My dad looked down at that cheap beige plastic button on the wrist of his collared shirt—you know, the ones that always chip or crack in the washer or dryer. He slowly dragged his fingers over the button as if he were grazing the corners of a circle. It seemed like two minutes had passed.

"I don't know, Kyle . . ." His mother had just died in a car accident.

I don't remember what I had asked him. As I sat there scrunched on the floor with my head between my legs, I could hear the suffering in his loss for words. I wanted to stand up and hug him. I wanted to squeeze him. I wanted to push all the sorrow in his gut up through his weary lungs and right out the top of his head. I wanted to fix him. I didn't know how to feel then and there, nor had I when my grandmother had passed away a year or two before. All I knew was silence. All I knew was to be silent.

"Just keep still . . . and watch what you say," I told myself. I was starting to sound like a mother. "Be careful with your words. In fact, just don't talk."

I was afraid to offend or hurt him with my innocent-but-ignorant questions for which he had no answer. So I just shut up. I clammed up and sat there in silence.

Putting Silence in Perspective

Why was I quiet? What do we understand by the word "silence"? What is silence? What does "being silent" mean? What does it look like to practice silence? How and why would this be important?

On a very basic level, silence is the absence of sound. But it's particularly easy for us to mistake real silence for fantastical silence—impossible silence. There are some forms of silence that we can never experience. For example, sometimes we talk about silence as the absence of all sounds; that is, silence means no noise is flooding our airwaves. But what we really mean often is the absence of another human voice. We mean that we don't hear anyone speaking—no one is babbling, uttering, talking, or engaging in other forms of verbal human communication.

The lack of human words, however, is not quite the absence of sound, is it? The music of sound is all around us. Every day the world utters sounds that we don't register. They are there, and they are "heard," but we become so accustomed to them that we don't single them out and hear them with awareness. In fact, a lot of sounds are uttered around us daily. When we stop talking, the world continues to speak and gesticulate. Trees whisper, flies buzz, raccoons chitter, and crows caw. Lilies wave, the sun smiles, fences dance, and the river claps its hands.

There is no silence. There is only the practicing of silence. When we "are" silent—when we practice silence—we deliberately shut up in a particular situation for a particular reason. When we practice this silence, we are putting our words to rest for a time or a season. It isn't that we can't or won't speak; we choose not to speak. This doesn't mean that we cut down on our speech or say a little less. No, we don't say anything at all. Or if we are physically incapable of speech, we practice silence by refraining from sign language or other methods of nonverbal communication. We refrain from intentionally having someone else (or even ourselves) take in our words or apprehend our communication. In short, to practice silence is to deliberately refrain from talking for certain reasons. Silence is about hearing our neighbor. It's about making space for her to contribute to our wisdom and our way of life. It's about talking just the right amount and balancing our listening and speaking.

If we look closely at our lived experience and practice of "being quiet," we will notice two things that can help us put silence in perspective. First, silence isn't a lack of communication. We speak with more than just our words. We can say things with our silence too, especially when we consider the time and the situation in which we are silent. When we are silent during a sermon or a funeral or a family feud, we are saying something with our silence. Second, the practice of silence isn't merely clamming up. Listening is also involved in our practice of silence. When we refrain from talking, we do so for others. We do it so that they can speak and so that we can listen to them. Silence is a way to "pass the mic" to others so that they can speak and be heard.

Loving Our Neighbor with Our Tongue and Words

Despite the popular conception, not many biblical passages address silence. And several of the passages that seem to discuss silence don't readily or necessarily translate to practicing silence, such as "being still" (*raphah*) and knowing God (Ps. 46:10). Despite this dearth of passages, many of us were taught that the spiritual discipline of silence goes hand in hand with solitude and that both are waysto get away from the world and spend time with God. In solitude we get away from the world, and in silence we listen to God. Both are practices that remove us from the noise of the world and enable us to hear God—because apparently God doesn't, won't, or can't speak quietly or amid noise.

Of course, while there is nothing wrong with taking time daily to listen to and hear from God, this notion may reduce the spiritual discipline of silence to something that it's not. We've missed one of its essential features. We've overlooked the important horizontal dimension to this practice. When we really think about it, and even take a look at our lived practice of "quiet time," which isn't the same as practicing silence but has some similarities, more is going on in the discipline of silence than we typically think of or see. Instead of being only an individual affair between us and God, silence can and does impact those around us in very concrete and practical ways.

As Christians, we are called to use our tongue and words to uplift others. The apostle Paul makes this plain in his letter to the church in Ephesus:

> You were taught to put away your former way of life, your old self, corrupt and deluded by its lusts, and to be renewed in the spirit of your minds, and to clothe yourselves with the new self, created according to the likeness of God in true righteousness and holiness.

So then, putting away falsehood, let all of us speak the truth to our neighbors, for we are members of one another. Be angry but do not sin; do not let the sun go down on your anger, and do not make room for the devil. Thieves must give up stealing; rather let them labor and work honestly with their own hands, so as to have something to share with the needy. Let no evil talk come out of your mouths, but only what is useful for building up, as there is need, so that your words may give grace to those who hear. And do not grieve the Holy Spirit of God, with which you were marked with a seal for the day of redemption. Put away from you all bitterness and wrath and anger and wrangling and slander, together with all malice, and be kind to one another, tenderhearted, forgiving one another, as God in Christ has forgiven you. (Eph. 4:22–32)

In short, let your words edify, reconcile, and heal. Don't speak ill of your neighbor; speak kindly. Don't tear your neighbor down; build her up. Use your tongue and words for good.

At the heart of solitude is the idea that as whole persons, our tongues and words belong to God. He is the Creator, Redeemer, and Restorer of these things too. He calls and commands us to steward these gifts in ways that lift up and love our neighbor and heal and harmonize our world. He calls and commands us to use our tongues and words for his purposes. God did not give us the gift of tongues, words, and voices to use selfishly, which we can and often do. Our voices, tongues, and words are not ours for our own enjoyment and purposes. Yes, they do benefit us. We can communicate and use our tongues and words to get what we want and need. But they were made for greater purposes than for us to simply talk, hear ourselves speak, or even communicate with others. French philosopher Jean-Louis Chrétien aptly remarks, "The voice is not an instrument for itself."[2] Our voices, tongues, and words (and other gifts of meaning and communication) have been given to us so that we can love our neighbor.

At times we use our words to deliberately and explicitly hurt others, as when we malign them. This is probably not the norm for most of us, though. Far more often we want to encourage and edify someone, but we say too much or our neighbor doesn't want to hear what we have to say. Our words are unwelcome. Or perhaps the eager Christian really wants to share the good news with his neighbor, but she doesn't want to hear it. Yet he insists and persists. His words are loving, but his actions are self-centered. It's in these moments of our daily lives that we lose control of our talking. We don't remember all the words we say. We say things at the wrong time or in the wrong way. We say things that we don't mean to say. The pressure of the moment and the weariness or demand of life can force us to say things we regret—we wish we could rewind time and just keep quiet.

We could use a little discipline in our talk. We could use a little control with our chattering. We need to tame our tongues and whip our words into shape. And we can do this through the practice of silence, which remedies selfish ways of talking. As a practice, which means that it is done regularly, it pushes back on selfish and sinful talking by getting us into a rhythm of hitting the "pause" button, which halts the spouting of words in our interaction with our neighbor. This, of course, is not the same as "going quiet" when things get heated. We are not just shutting up to avoid conflict or to let our neighbor say something that we wait to refute. We are clamming up so we can hear our neighbor, so that we can better understand her, so we can make space for her, and so that we can perhaps, in some cases, hear more in order to resolve the conflict present in our community. Practicing silence leads us to discipline our mouths and tongues so that we can fix our malformed habits of talking in community and helps us develop habits that resist excessive talking and harmful speech, which may otherwise come out of us in the heat of the moment.

We aren't just physical bodies that inhabit space in harmful ways; we are talking bodies that can inhabit "verbal space" in harmful ways. It's important for us not to let our talking drown out others. A good rule of thumb is what the Countess of Rousillon says in act 1, scene 1 of Shakespeare's *All's Well That Ends Well*: "Be check'd for silence, but never tax'd for speech."[3] The practice of silence is an agent of healing in a world of harmful words and wordiness. Over time its practice makes the practice of listening more frequent and maybe even a little more desirable. Disciplining our tongue and withholding our words help us get comfortable being silent. We gain some control over how much we respond and how quickly, especially as we practice this again and again. Over time, we train our tongue to wait a second. We learn to appreciate and practice slow speech. We get into the habit of controlling ourselves in the moment and filtering the words that we are thinking in the moment but probably shouldn't say.

In a world of ubiquitous earbud use, flashy billboards, and less than two-minute attention spans, surely the daily practice of silence would be an act of love toward our neighbor. Going even further, in a world of selfish, opinionated "chatterboxes" who are entertained and amused by political pundits talking over each other on the news, the simple practice of being quiet and truly listening to another person is an act of love. The practice of silence truly is a countercultural practice because it institutes self-denial in speech and invites and welcomes the words of others. It values the words of others. It wants to hear from them. It fosters auditory hospitality.[4] Because of this, it is a sacrificial act. In the grand scheme of things, it is what makes a community become people who are swift to hear and slow to speak (James 1:19).

Do we love our neighbor if we never allow her to reveal herself because we are always chattering? Do we love our neighbor if we do not permit her to share her wisdom and insight because our "auditory airwaves" are always flooded with our own voice? How can we love our neighbor if we don't hear her words and heed them? How can we truly edify and empower her if we don't let her speak? We should love our neighbor with our words by edifying and empowering her, as the apostle Paul encourages us. But we should also love our neighbor by withholding our words. To talk as the apostle Paul invites us to talk in the way of Jesus involves uplifting others in our speech and taking time to listen to others. The practice of silence can help us do both of these things—charitable speaking and hospitable listening, which is the way that Jesus spoke. In North American democratic society, it may be that silence before our neighbor is a greater service to her well-being and a greater act of love toward her than anything that we have to say.

If we truly want to love our neighbor as ourselves, we need to change how we talk around and about our neighbor. If we are to move from mere membership in a talking community to fellowship as edifying talkers, we need to pay attention to our priorities and practices of talking. For most of us, we probably need to change how frequently we talk to our neighbor. Some of us may need to talk to her for the first time. Others may need to reconcile with her. We can't love our neighbor if we hurt her with our words and if we bombard her with so many words that she can't offer her own. I think I speak for all of us when I say that we could do a better job of loving our neighbor with our mouths and words. Disciplining our mouths and tongues through the discipline of silence would be another small but significant way that we could love our neighbor with our daily deeds and everyday activities.

Side Steps: Silence

Prayer

Father, we are grateful for mouths, tongues, and throats to utter, babble, speak, shout, and sing, and we are grateful for our hands, arms, and bodies that we use also to communicate with others. We are grateful that we can communicate with others to share advice, encouragement, and warnings. Yet we acknowledge that we frequently use these devices for our own glory and to our neighbor's grief. Jesus, redeem our gift of talking and speaking so that our words can bring healing and harmony to the world. May our words build up your kingdom and invite your reign. Spirit, guide us to choose our words wisely. Help us discern when it is appropriate to silence ourselves so that others may speak and we may listen. In Jesus's name we pray. Amen.

Simple Steps to Practice Silence

- If you're a homemaker, try to make silence part of the daily rhythm in your home. I do this with my kids on my days off (we call it "quiet time"). For a whole hour we don't talk—sign language, written notes, gestures, and pointing are permitted. If you're at work five or six days a week, try practicing silence during lunchtime. If it's nearly impossible to be silent during the day or at night, try to make listening more of your interaction with others than speaking. If that's not possible, try to refrain from talking about yourself. Deflect the focus from yourself.

- Try practicing silence in public places. It's kind of awkward, but it's also rewarding. One time I did this with close friends at a pub late at night. We wrote on a napkin to communicate with our waiter. To resist technological "talking" and avoidance of one another, we both put our phones on the table. First one to reach for his phone had to foot the bill.

- If you're a parent, a good time to practice silence is before bed. Something that's worked in the Bennett household is our practice, before bed, of doing our "Four Ts." The kids brush their *teeth*, use the *toilet*, grab a *tissue*, and then we *talk*. Our talking time consists of five questions: When did you feel most happy today? When did you feel most miserable? Did you feel guilty at any point? What are you grateful for today? What did you learn about yourself and your world? There is no "talk-back"—so the kids really learn the importance of being silent and listening to others.

- Another convenient time to practice silence is when you practice meditation, solitude, service, Sabbath keeping, or fasting. Keep that in mind. Remember: repetition and regularity. We're trying to make these practices part of our daily deeds.

SEVEN

HOW TO MAKE FRIENDS
AND EMPOWER PEOPLE

SERVICE AND RENEWED WORKING

When I was in college and decided that I wanted to tie the knot, I knew I needed a ring to do it. But in order to get a ring, I needed a job. Not just any job but one that fit with my basketball schedule and was in close proximity to the school. I preferred it to be something that didn't require much mental effort, you know, given my studies. Wendy's fit the bill. So did Home Depot. But for whatever reason, I decided on Subway. For a young undergrad, the perks were amiable. "Free meals, and we can be quite flexible scheduling your hours," they told me. Sold. Two days later, I was walking in November snow from school to Subway to shadow one of the other employees.

Things were going well until I met the manager on my first evening shift. It was either the angle or the incline of the doorway, but I couldn't even see him when he entered. He was so vertically challenged he didn't even make it above industrial-grade counters. Well, that was until I realized that he wasn't vertically challenged—he was just undeveloped. A smoked-out wannabe-skater with muddy gold hair that coddled his earlobes, frayed tan Dickies, and squeaky-clean black Doc Martens, the evening shift manager was a chunky pile of frustration. Here I was almost a college graduate taking terse, aggressive orders from some pipsqueak high school student. I still don't know how I managed to endure those three to four months.

He frequently poked fun at me, but not the kind of strange jests and jabs that strangers throw at one another in the hope of coming to some final conflict where they can have a genuine heart-to-heart and become besties. No, this was the kind that hurt. Time and again, it almost led to altercations. As a manager, he wasn't a likable guy, and he definitely didn't empower me. As a coworker, he had to show me weekly that I didn't know aaaaanyyyyything about throwing meat and lettuce on stale bread. I'm sure you've met a few miserable miscreants in your lifetime, but in my world, he was by far the worst coworker ever. When the final paycheck came that sealed the deal for the ring, I busted out of that joint.

Like owning, thinking, eating, socializing, and talking, working is basic to being human and functioning as a human being. We labor, toil, and put effort into something every day. Even if we're unemployed, we work every day. Like all things human, the work we do every day is done in community and with the help of community. Someone taught us how to do what we do at our nine-to-five and what we do when we come home from our nine-to-five. Someone taught us what to do in our cubicle and how and where to put things in our cupboard. We have coworkers who work alongside us to accomplish the tasks and responsibilities that we have to do. All our work is informed by the work of others and the quality of that work, and our work shapes and impacts the work of others.

If we take a close look at how we labor and put effort into everything that we do, many of us will agree that our working habits and practices tend to be selfish or self-centered. Instead of working for or with our neighbor, we work against her. We may not do so in a malicious way, but we make work about ourselves and acquiring the things that we want, doing the things we find beneficial, and getting the accolades that we desire. I want to single out two tendencies in work habits and practices in our North American democratic culture that, to some degree, hurt our neighbor and negatively impact her livelihood: negligent working and competitive working. Although they might seem minor, and therefore harmless, this kind of selfish work in our cubicles, offices, and kitchens can damage our interpersonal relationship with our neighbor and our life in community.

Malformed Working: Neglecting Our Workload and Others

One way we tend toward selfish working is by neglecting to do our workload and properly attend to our coworkers.

Diligence means giving something the proper care and attention that it deserves, and sometimes even delighting in doing so. Something is worthy of our consideration, supervision, protection, or help, so we tend to it as we should. We are assiduous in our dealings with it. Negligence is the opposite of diligence. It is to not give something the proper care and attention that it deserves. It is to not pick up something that should be picked up or to disregard something that ought to be regarded. It is to not be assiduous with something that demands attention. So instead of supervising, nurturing, or protecting something that warrants or needs it, the negligent person attends to something else that, presumably, he holds in higher regard or delight.

Negligence is not ignorance, however. To be negligent, a person must have knowledge. He must know that he is dealing with something that is worth his attention and care, and with this knowledge he chooses not to give it his attention and care. He chooses to disregard the thing, most likely in order to attend to something else. He is fully aware that he ought to do otherwise, but he chooses to neglect it. The ignorant person, however, doesn't know that something is worth his attention and care, so he doesn't give it. He isn't technically making a decision because there is no choice for him. He doesn't do something because he doesn't know he should. Choosing not to pick something up that one knows is worth picking up is very different from not knowing something's worth and whether one should pick it up. In other words, the negligent person isn't ignorant, and the ignorant person isn't negligent. One doesn't know any better; the other does know better, but he just doesn't care.

Negligent work habits and practices can show up in two broad ways. First, we can be negligent with our workload. We can neglect the duties and responsibilities that we are expected to fulfill or are employed to do at our nine-to-five job. So, for example, we choose not to do that report for our boss, who expects us to complete it by the end of the week. If we chose not to do this report, we are neglecting our workload. Or suppose we are expected to say a few remarks at a very important honor society meeting Monday evening, but we choose to go to the pub instead. We neglect to do our share in this project or event. Perhaps we neglect our work because we're lazy, slacking off, or just detest the kind of tasks we are required to do. In these examples, we have neglected to do our share of the workload.

We can also be negligent with our coworkers. This may seem strange, but we can neglect to attend to our colleagues, partners, or team in the way that they expect us to as coworkers on a common task or project. Having pints with colleagues or congratulating someone for winning Employee of the Month may not be in our job description or high on our priorities list; however, we all know from personal experience that decisions, gestures, and deeds like

these impact our relationship with our coworkers, our work environment, and our team's productivity. If we don't collaborate with
a coworker, forgo hanging out after work, or fail to celebrate her
achievements or birthday, she will likely feel neglected. She may
not feel respected as a colleague or even as a person. There will be
times, of course, when we forget or get wrapped up with something
else. Honest mistakes happen. But this kind of oversight is quite
different from choosing to not care for or attend to our coworker.

Negligence is not a type of work but a malformed way to work.
This isn't the way that Jesus worked, and it isn't the way that Jesus
calls and commands us to work. It's a selfish way to work. We can
and should love our neighbor with our hands and labor, but we are
not doing so when we neglect her or our workload. Both forms of
negligence are insensitive and hurtful to our neighbor. Such negligence doesn't take seriously the fact that we have a responsibility
to others in, with, and through our work. We are part of a team and
a common project. When we don't step up to the plate and do the
job, others are affected. Negligence with respect to our coworkers
doesn't take seriously the fact that our colleagues are our neighbors.
They are the neighbors that we are called to love. How can we love
our neighbor if we don't see our neighbor at work? How can we love
our neighbor if we don't help her with her work, and do our work,
which is also part of her work?

Malformed Working: Competing with Others

We also tend to be selfish in our work by competing with others.
Whether we are educators, sales reps, politicians, or truck drivers, our work involves others to some degree. We teach students
alongside colleagues. We sell to consumers with others on a sales
team. We legislate law with others in a congress. We supply goods
to retailers and drive one delivery route among many. All work

is done with, from, and in community. We work for others, with others, and because of others. So on many levels, we need others in order to do our jobs. We need others to help us do what we do, and we do what we do so that others can receive, use, or consume something they need.

Though few of us are professional athletes, our work tends to become a competition. We work with others, yet we compete with them for accolades and accomplishments—we want that Employee of the Month plaque, promotion, or salary increase. The competition isn't friendly, though, that's for sure. When we compete with others in this way, our goal isn't to spur one another on to better practices or greater proficiency. We're not trying to better one another. Our intention is not to motivate others to do better work. Rather, more often than not, our goal is to win. It's survival of the fittest out here, and we're trying to keep this job . . . and make others jealous. Or we're hoping to move on to bigger and better things.

To hold a contest or to challenge someone in a task is different from competing with her. Contests and challenges are primarily about fostering excellence. They are about testing limits and developing abilities. At work, contests and challenges can be motivating factors. They can build up community and encourage personal and professional development. To hold a contest or challenge one another doesn't set up such opposition. There is a sense of friendly striving for the betterment of all. But to compete is to contend for something against others. It is to pursue some kind of prize and intentionally come into conflict with another person. Competition always leads to clashing and colliding as one pursues a prize. It intentionally sets one competitor in opposition to another. A competition encourages a sense of opposition, victory, and defeat.

Competitive working is not a type of work but a malformed way to work. It wasn't the way Jesus worked, and it isn't the way Jesus calls us to work. He didn't compete with others, and I don't believe that Jesus invites us to compete with others in this way. Like negligence, it's a selfish way to work. It leads to conflict and even hostility among colleagues. Perhaps more insidiously, competitive working makes the work that we do primarily about victories and prizes, achievements and accolades. Our job becomes a place and a time for us to show what we can do and to "win." This might even come at the expense of doing our job and meeting our responsibilities well. It makes work about getting something (such as a reward), or showing something to others (such as our gifts or talents), rather than participating in and completing the work well.

We can and should love our neighbor with our hands and work, but we are not doing so when we compete against her. Work is not about getting our name on a plaque or receiving a promotion. (Although if we do get that promotion as a result of good work, who can complain! But the end for which we work should not be the promotion.) It's not about personal achievements, accomplishments, and advancements. When the work we do becomes a competition and the workplace becomes a dog-eat-dog environment, our effort becomes a way to defeat our neighbor and tear her down instead of helping her, building her up, and working together. We work against her, not for and with her. That is not the way of Jesus, and that is not how we can and should love our neighbor with our work.

Service and Renewed Working

Remember the story of Martha and Mary in the Gospel of Luke? The story goes that Martha welcomes Jesus into her home and her sister Mary sits at Jesus's feet listening to him while Martha continues working. This apparently frustrates Martha, and she asks Jesus to tell Mary to help her. Jesus says, "Martha, Martha, you are worried and distracted by many things; there is need of only one thing. Mary has chosen the better part, which will not be taken away from her" (Luke 10:41–42).

When we first heard this story, many of us were probably told that Martha is preparing a meal for Jesus and Mary isn't helping. As an apparent resident of the hosting home, Mary should be helping her sister Martha cook dinner, not just sitting there listening. How inconsiderate! How rude! Mary is enjoying herself, while Martha is putting in all the effort! But then Jesus does something unexpected: he flips it on Martha. He seems to chastise Martha and imply that learning is more important than working, that being with people is more important than doing stuff for them, or that communing with the Lord is more commendable than doing tasks for him.

For me, this story says something else. It says something about service and what the practice of service really looks like. Many of us probably want to be Mary. We aspire to sit at our Lord's feet. We want to soak up every word Jesus is saying, even if we don't fully understand all of them. We just want to be with him. But I think that if Jesus ever visited our home, we wouldn't be anything close to Mary. We would totally be Martha. We'd be running around the house picking up laundry, wiping mud off the carpet, centering pictures, refilling the water filter, straightening the sheets, and sweeping the dust bunnies. We'd be baking cookies and making lemonade. I don't know what Martha was thinking or doing, but I do know that time and time again, I am Martha. I can't stop being Martha. I care so much about doing things for others that I tend to overlook my company. I get caught up with doing things for others that I think are important to them.

Maybe you're a bit like me. Are there times in your life when you're so concerned with helping others with what you think will help them that you're totally oblivious to what they want or need from you? Are there times when your help is motivated by a concern to keep face, maintain a reputation, or impress others rather than a genuine desire to actually help or minister to them? I don't know what Martha was thinking or doing. But I do know that there are times when I'm not really thinking of my neighbor; I'm thinking about what my neighbor will think of me. I'm not really helping my neighbor; I'm doing what I think will help her. Secretly, deep, deep down, what I'm really trying to do is control how I help my neighbor. I'm helping her, which is great, but more often than not, I'm doing it in a way that's unhelpful to her.

Putting Service in Perspective

As Christians, we are called, commanded, and commissioned to love and serve our neighbor. Jesus and the apostle Paul, and the entire biblical narrative, make this clear:

> But Jesus called them to him and said, "You know that the rulers of the Gentiles lord it over them, and their great ones are tyrants over them. It will not be so among you; but whoever wishes to be great among you must be your servant, and whoever wishes to be first among you must be your slave [*doulos*]." (Matt. 20:25–27)

> For you were called to freedom, brothers and sisters; only do not use your freedom as an opportunity for self-indulgence, but through love become slaves [*doulos*] to one another. (Gal. 5:13)

Christians are commissioned to serve. But what exactly does this mean? What does it mean not to lord it over someone? What does it mean to be a servant? What does service look like? At its most basic level, service is a form of work. It involves toiling and putting in effort. But like the other disciplines we've discussed in this book, the spiritual discipline of service is often misunderstood. It differs uniquely from other kinds of labor and effort.

Two kinds of service are worth mentioning: assistance and doing a favor. To assist someone is to come alongside him and help him with a task. Suppose I see a man carrying boxes on the street. He trips over the curb and drops one or all of them. I run across the street to help him. In this situation I would be assisting him. And, of course, we all know what it means to do someone a favor. It is to help someone with a task or do the task for him. What we don't often realize is that many times we have the expectation that there will be some return or reward for our act of kindness. We anticipate or hope for a return on our favor. We assume that the other person will reciprocate at some point. For example, I help a friend move with the expectation that he will help me when I move.

If Jesus is our model for understanding service, we can conclude from his life and death that merely assisting another person or doing her a favor with the expectation of some return is not quite the act of service Jesus had in mind. Service is more than merely assisting someone in a time of inconvenience or difficulty, and it definitely isn't doing something for someone with the expectation of return or reward. Rather, service involves actively seeking out ways to help others, not waiting for them to screw up what they're doing and then running to help them. It also intentionally sacrifices any benefit or reward. It involves humbly stepping down from a position of power and authority and doing a radical act that in no way benefits us (John 13:15). There's no reward to be sought in service beyond the sheer pleasure of loving another human being and living in a way that witnesses to Jesus.

Fresh out of college I got a job as a youth and associate pastor at a church plant in Florida. Each of the two years I was there, our congregation would walk through the neighborhood on Christmas Eve, knock on people's doors, and politely ask them if they needed anything this holiday season. While I knew it was a kind gesture, I always felt it was a bit intrusive, maybe even a bit aggressive. But that's probably because I don't like this kind of approach myself. Call me a budding curmudgeon, but I don't like people knocking on my door late in the evening, whether it's Halloween trick-or-treaters or Christmas carolers. And I certainly don't enjoy doing it to others.

Knocking on doors wouldn't have been my idea of serving the community, that's for sure. Despite being anxious every time we did it, I was always pleasantly surprised by how well it was received. Sure, a few doors went an inch ajar and then closed, but none of these doors were slammed shut. Most people were delighted to have someone offer to help them. Quite a few wanted weeds plucked. A few needed furniture moved. Some asked for prayer. Some inquired if we knew any Christmas carols. As I thought about it over the years, I realized that this awkward, anxiety-inducing activity was actual service (even though we did it only once a year). Over time I've learned that what we want for our neighbor and what our neighbor wants or needs from us are often not the same.

Loving Our Neighbor with Our Hands and Labor

Most of us brought up in the Christian tradition were taught that the spiritual discipline of service is a kind of project we do for those who are homeless—literally. We grew up serving at the soup kitchen one night a month or going on an annual mission trip to a so-called third world country to build a home. Once a month or once a year, we took time out of our schedule to go somewhere outside our neighborhood and help others. That was service for us.

While this kind of effort is valuable, and we should help others whenever we can and with whatever means we can, I don't think that building a home once a year or pouring soup into a bowl once a month is what Jesus had in mind when he invited us to serve one another. We've reduced this discipline and flattened it to fit what we are willing to put into it. Maybe helping someone once a month or once a year is the beginning of service, but it's certainly not its end. We've overlooked something important in the practice of service. We've missed a much deeper dimension and calling to our neighbor through the practice of service. Is service just a shotgun act of help? Is it an annual, one-time deal? Have we reached our quota with just one day a year of serving the community? Or is there more to service?

If we look at the big picture of Jesus's life (and death), we see that Jesus didn't serve only once in a while; he served all the time. What does that mean? He sacrificed for others. He devoted himself to the needs and healing of others (Matt. 25:34–40). He disregarded his own interests and "worked" for others (Luke 22:27). He labored and put in effort to make things better for others as whole persons. He even willingly subjected himself to their sin, foolishness, and evil. He served in this way for his entire life and with his entire life (Matt. 20:28). He served through more than simply doing big projects. He didn't meet his "service quota" by building a home once a year or pouring soup into a bowl once a month. His life and death were run through with service. He didn't wait for others to call him; he actively sought out ways to help others. He made it his mission to love, heal, and reconcile. He did this with everything that he had, every time he had the chance (Gal. 5:13). He didn't force his help on others or force them to accept the kind of help he thought they needed. In a consistently incarnational posture, he met them where they were and helped them where they were and with what they needed. And he did this daily.

What do you do daily? What consumes most of your time and energy? To what end do you toil? Where do you put in effort? What constitutes the majority of your daily deeds? Chemical engineering? Banking? Producing films? Coding? Waiting tables? Watching the kids? All these activities involve others. Other people make our jobs possible, and they are necessary for our work. Needless to say, many people benefit from our work. The banker helps people save, secure, and manage money. The producer helps people relax after a long day. The waitress helps people get food promptly and efficiently in a crowded, busy restaurant.

Every day we have things to do at our job, but we also have other work to do. When we get home, we have to clean up the kitchen, fix the car, or compile the church bulletin. All these tasks are important, and they, too, indirectly or directly benefit others. A clean kitchen keeps everyone safe and healthy. A repaired car is a date-night vehicle and a reliable source of transportation for friends and family. A completed bulletin helps busy parishioners feel connected. Whatever we do affects others—which is why it's important to do it well. We can love and serve our neighbor through our daily work just by doing these tasks and fulfilling our responsibilities well. When we do so, we provide material or immaterial goods for our neighbor that will preserve and protect her life or make it more comfortable and peaceful. This service is a good thing.

Our labor and effort extend far beyond what we do from nine in the morning to five in the evening. Employment is only one form of work. We cannot draw a hard and fast line between the kinds of work we do because God certainly doesn't. There may be distinct ways of working, but they all come under the umbrella of work.[1] Whenever we are doing an activity, we are working. And if we look close enough, we will see that we have plenty of opportunities to love and serve our neighbor in our daily activities. But it's tough, isn't it? The hustle and bustle of our lives can make serious demands on our time and energy. These two things become our most prized possessions. Very few of us like sharing them with others—unless, of course, these others are part of how we want to spend our free time and energy!

More often than not, we tend to spend our free time and energy on things that benefit us. We do things on the side that result in compensation or some kind of reward. If there isn't monetary gain involved, or we're not doing something for sheer pleasure, then we do it because it will boost our reputation or the favor will come in handy someday. We usually don't want to spend our evenings and weekends serving or helping others. But we can and should love our neighbor beyond what we are required to do every day at work. Perhaps this involves helping her with her tasks and responsibilities at home. Or maybe it means helping to reduce her load at school functions. We can and should help her when we're at our job, but we should also serve her when we're off the clock, so to speak.

We could use some direction. We could use some discipline with respect to our hands. We need to control our working and working patterns. We need a way to become more aware of others in order to help them through our daily deeds. As contemporary theologian Norman Wirzba rightly says, "We need to consider how the work we perform either nurtures or violates the integrity of the places in which our work has effects, and carefully note if what we do contributes to the overall health of communities and regions."[2] In general, we need to consider how our work impacts others, and we need to consider working outside our job to impact others in ways that bring health and healing. This is what we strive for in the discipline of service.

Service is a practice that remedies and renews selfish working. It helps others. It makes others a priority in our lives—even when doing so is difficult or inconvenient. When we practice service, we push back on malformed ways of working. It disciplines us to re-direct time and energy from our busy schedules or free time—filled with personal interests, goals, and responsibilities—to help other members in our communities flourish and have a sustainable living alongside us. We make our neighbor's well-being as important as our own livelihood. In our service we take steps to go from membership to fellowship. Though it may seem small and even worthless in a dog-eat-dog culture, not treating your colleague like a competitor or a villain is an act of love toward her. Treating her as one of your teammates whom you help and serve is an act of love. In a culture where "me time" is sacred and untouchable, spending time with her outside work is also an act of love. It shows her that we love her enough to inconvenience ourselves and shift our schedules for her.

At the heart of service is the idea that our time, energy, hands, and goals belong to God. He is the Creator, Redeemer, and Restorer of these, too. God calls and commands us to steward these gifts in ways that lift up our neighbor, express love, and heal and harmonize our world. He calls us to use our hands and work for his purposes. We can love others by doing our work well and by treating our neighbor at work well. We can work alongside her to help and benefit her and others. At work, we can love and serve her through our daily tasks and responsibilities, but we can also love our neighbor by simply making small adjustments to our habits and practices of working. By making the practice of service a part of our daily deeds and thereby making slight changes to our daily work, we can help and heal our neighbor in and through the little things.

We are busy people, but we can carve out time from our daily deeds to serve others and make service to others a part of each day. We can make serving our neighbor part of the rhythm of our daily work, just like Jesus did.

If we truly want to love our neighbor as ourselves, we need to change how we work with and for our neighbor. We need to change how we relate to her as a coworker, and we need to change the way we work so that we actually work to help her. We need to love her with our hands and labor. If we are to move from membership to fellowship at work, we need to pay attention to our work priorities and practices. We need to see the selfish priorities in our existing practices and reconfigure these priorities by changing these practices. This is one small but significant way that we can love our neighbor with our daily deeds and everyday activities. Consistently and frequently using our hands to help those in need will help us love our neighbor as ourselves.

Side Steps: Service

Prayer

Provider of all things, your hand gives to those in need even when they don't recognize your help or thank you for your gift. You are patient, generous, and thoughtful in your work. May we help others as you do. May we work with the same care, consistency, and closeness as you do. Help us to lay down our lives to serve others and work for their benefit as your Son did. Holy Spirit, give us the strength to serve when we are tired after a long week. Grant us the motivation to serve when we are irritable and distracted by other things in our life, and give us the opportunity to serve our neighbor daily in the smaller corridors of our lives—in the kitchen, in our cubicle, or at the pub. In Jesus's name we pray. Amen.

Simple Steps to Practice Service

- As much as possible, we should strive to make service part of our daily rhythm—five minutes, thirty minutes, or an hour. If you commute to work, offer to drive a carpool. If you are a teacher, offer a free seminar or book study over lunch. Think long and hard about what those around you need and how you might be able to help them.

- If you're at work from nine to five, a convenient time to serve is during your lunch break. But take into account who you are and who is around you. Are you a night owl? Can you serve others in the evening after work? Are you up at the crack of dawn? Can you help anyone in the mornings for a few minutes? Know yourself and look around for ways to serve.

- If you're a stay-at-home parent, and your kids are of age, plan a weekly service project on Fridays. Go serve at the soup kitchen. Helping your kids acquire a rhythm of service once a week is better than once a month or once a year.

- Start close and small. Ask your friends and neighbors if you can help them with anything: "How are you? Is there anything you need?" Then ask acquaintances or strangers whom you regularly see if there is anything you can do for them. If you see them in need, ask if you can help.

EIGHT

WORK HARD, CONSECRATE HARD

SABBATH KEEPING AND RENEWED RESTING

For me, it was a youth lock-in when I was in high school. A friend was doing a youth event at his church, and foolish me crashed the party to get pied in the face and eat fish eyes. The first night I slogged it out by playing video games all night and crushing Mountain Dew. It was epic and terribly foolish. I woke up around eight o'clock the following evening. Apparently I had fallen asleep on the couch while eating dinner. I couldn't remember half the morning or any of the afternoon. Thirty-two hours of Christian debauchery will do that to you.

Maybe you've never done a youth lock-in, but you know a thing or two about crashing. You have newborns. Your brother has insomnia. Your roommates like to party. You have a toddler with epilepsy. We all know the value of rest. But if our lived experience isn't enough, sleep experts tell us that we need rest in order to process information. Our brains go into cognitive overload, and we can't synthesize information unless we rest. Athletic trainers and physicians will tell us that to be healthy and strong we need to give our bodies a break. If we lift weights every day, we'll tear muscle tissue beyond repair. If we run every day, we may put too much stress on bones, tendons, or ligaments. Our bodies need rest and so do our minds.

Supposedly sleeping, taking lunch breaks, going on vacation, taking sick days or maternity or paternity leave, or going on a sabbatical help us rest. But as many of us have experienced time and again, we don't actually get any rest when we do these activities, do we? We often find ourselves still working on these planned escapes from work. We check our email on vacation, or we take a sabbatical to write a book. We don't rest. We don't feel rested afterward. Some of us just don't value rest in the way we should: "I'll rest when I'm dead," we say. Workaholism is alive in our North American democratic culture. We work too much. As a result, many of us don't rest as much as we should. We get four hours of sleep a night, maybe six, but experience teaches us that rest is something we need as human beings.

The Bible teaches us that God made us with the ability to and need for rest. That's why we crash when we don't rest. But we may not realize that in the Bible God also commands us to rest (Exod. 20:8–11). God tells us that we must rest (Exod. 23:12). And in commanding it, God explains what it means to rest—truly rest. When we look closely at what God has to say about it, we realize that our expressions of rest are not the kind of rest God commands (Matt. 11:28; Josh. 21:44–45). Our misunderstanding and lack of true rest have implications not only for our health and vitality but also for our neighbor's livelihood.

We rest because God rests. The Bible tells us that from the very beginning God rested.

> The heavens and the earth were finished, and all their multitude. And on the seventh day God finished the work that he had done,

and he rested on the seventh day from all the work that he had done. So God blessed the seventh day and hallowed it, because on it God rested from all the work that he had done in creation. (Gen. 2:1–3)

Perhaps the most obvious point in this passage is that an infinite, powerful God rested. Yeah, that's kind of crazy, isn't it? That seems so counterintuitive. Why would someone without limits need or want to rest? He didn't need to, did he? It's not like he was tired. Well, then, maybe he wanted to do so. But why would he want to rest? What's so desirable about rest for someone who doesn't need it? And what did he "do" on the seventh day? Let's step back for just a second. What is rest? What does it mean to rest? What does it mean to rest from work? Is it possible to rest without resting from work?

The Bible tells us that God ceased (*shabbat*) doing something and rested. He created a bunch of stuff, finished up with it, and then stopped and rested. He then took an entire "day" to rest. He took a day off. And just before this day, he stepped back and evaluated: "God saw everything that he had made, and indeed, it was very good. And there was evening and there was morning, the sixth day" (Gen. 1:31). God took a look at his work. He saw it. He reflected on it. He considered it a job well done. He delighted in it. Later on in this story, we are told that God commands his people to rest as he rested.

> Remember the sabbath day, and keep it holy. Six days you shall labor and do all your work. But the seventh day is a sabbath to the LORD your God; you shall not do any work—you, your son or your daughter, your male or female slave, your livestock, or the alien resident in your towns. For in six days the LORD made heaven and earth, the sea, and all that is in them, but rested the seventh day; therefore the LORD blessed the sabbath day and consecrated it. (Exod. 20:8–11)

When we make resting about us and what *we* want to do to rejuvenate ourselves, our resting habits and practices become selfish and self-centered. If we're honest with ourselves, we aren't rejuvenated by these acts of rest, and in fact they drain our neighbor and hurt her on various levels. There are two resting habits in our North American democratic culture that we tend to practice: laziness and what I call "otherworking." Just as we can hurt others with our pockets and possessions, heads and thoughts, tummies and urges, tongues and words, shadows and presences, hands and work, we can hurt our neighbor with our rest. As we will see, we can hurt her by not sitting on our bums and truly resting, and we can hurt her by lying on our backs and not doing anything when we rest.

Malformed Resting: Being Lazy

"What's the laziest animal you know, Papa?"

My daughter (eight years old) had recently seen the Walt Disney film *Zootopia* (2016) and was smiling as she recollected the scene with Flash, the sloth DMV worker. "What's the laziest animal?" It isn't a question I get asked every day, so to be honest, I was a bit thrown off.

"I don't know," I said. "Let's Google it!" (By the way, how does one explain the internet and search engines to an eight-year-old? Do tell when you find out.)

We scrolled through memes, GIFs, images, and articles. She pointed to a koala. Koalas sleep anywhere from eighteen to twenty-two hours a day. Sleeping all the time—that seems kind of lazy, doesn't it? Sloths sleep a lot too. And, of course, they're so slooooooooooooooooowwwww. Sleepy and slow—now we're getting something. But then we saw some owls. "Don't owls just sit on branches all day and ask the same question—who?" "Well, I think that's just what people think," I told her. "Apparently they hunt and do other stuff."

"Oh! Frogs!" What do frogs do, exactly, besides croak and eat? Or bats? Hippos? Cats?

To be honest, the more I thought about it, I didn't really know which were lazy and which were just inactive. Does mere inactivity constitute laziness? If it can move but doesn't, does that make it lazy? In fact, I wondered if any of these animals or creatures could be considered lazy at all. Can nonhumans be lazy? Our research continues, I told her.

Laziness means being idle or languid. Something appears to be taking it slow or not moving at all. But when we use this word, we typically mean that someone or something is choosing to be idle. Many things display a lack of exertion and effort, but they are not being lazy. A rock. A frog. Maybe even a sloth. Laziness is choosing to be idle when one could be active. This, of course, is very different from being unable to do something. The person suffering from an illness who can't get out of bed or the disabled person who cannot walk is not lazy. Sickness, fatigue, and incapacity are not the stuff of laziness. In contrast, the lazy person is healthy and able to do activities, but he chooses to be idle instead (which, going back to chapter 7, is different from being negligent). Of course, we are all lazy at one time or another. But a lazy person is someone who consistently and frequently chooses not to do things that he is able to do.

We can be lazy in our work. We don't want to do the project that's due at the end of the day, so we just sit there and stare at our computer screen. We can also be lazy in our rest. All we want to do is come home, sit on the couch, and veg out all weekend. But if we pay attention to the result of our laziness, we find that it doesn't always lead to rest, does it? Have you ever stayed on the couch for an entire day? How did you feel when you got up that evening or the next morning? Have you ever vegged out all weekend after a long week at work? When you arrived at your desk on Monday morning, how did you feel? Lousy? Sluggish? Did you actually feel rested, rejuvenated, or refreshed?

Laziness is not a type of resting but a malformed way to rest. That's why it doesn't do for us what we want and expect from it. Jesus rested differently, and he calls and commands us to rest differently too. Laziness is a selfish way to rest. We can and should love our neighbor with our rest, but we are not doing so when we are lazy. Given that we find ourselves in concentric circles of community, when we are lazy during times of rest, we often disregard our neighbors. When we try to rest like this, we are unmotivated to consider or help her. We want to be left alone. Our vegging out makes our resting time untouchable to her. More often than not, though, we still have obligations to her (and to others), and she has expectations of us. Being lazy can disregard our neighbor, disrupt our communion with her, and damage possibilities for loving her.

Malformed Resting: "Otherworking"

Another way we tend to be selfish in our resting is by "otherworking." There are overworkers—those who work too many hours a week at their job—and then there are what I call "otherworkers." Otherworking is not truly rest at all, and it can find expression in many ways. One way that we otherwork is by physically bringing work home with us to do over the weekend. We don't end up resting; we just work from home. Another way that we otherwork is when we don't physically bring work home with us, but we do mentally. We spend our two weekend days thinking and worrying about Monday morning, when we return to our nine-to-five jobs. We spend our day(s) of rest being cognitively drained by the same stuff that burdens or, for some, boosts us throughout the week. We don't truly rest from our work—we just bring it home with us.

This otherworking can take another form as well. When we rest from our "employment" or our nine-to-five job, but we don't take a break from other tasks, responsibilities, labors, and efforts that demand our attention at home, we are otherworking. We spend the weekend diving into other tasks and responsibilities that consume our time and energy. This is the most common form of otherworking. Of course, there are gradations to this habit. The most extreme case might be spring-cleaning that isn't limited to springtime. We dust, clean the oven, wipe out the refrigerator, and rearrange the garage every weekend. A less extreme case might be that we always get a jump start on the reading for next week or prep for classes on Monday.

Otherworkers work too much, but not at their nine-to-five job like overworkers. If we are an otherworker, we are constantly working—at our job, at home, and everywhere else we go. We clean the house for fun. We play a show at the local pub. We do a stand-up set in the city. Because we don't see the bigger picture of work, which we discussed in the previous chapter, we tend to confuse our nine-to-five job with work altogether. We tend to think that we only need to rest from our nine-to-five. Not only this, but we find these other projects pleasurable and relaxing, so we don't consider them work.

The reality is that these activities are work, and they continue to drain us. Planning the upcoming week, doing household chores, and running errands are very important activities, but they do not foster rest. So we come home on the weekend (or our days off) and end up doing more work, which we don't really see as "work." We might even be very disciplined about not thinking, worrying, or planning for our nine-to-five job this upcoming week, but we still throw ourselves into mundane and seemingly innocuous stuff that we don't count as "work," but all we've really done is substitute one kind of labor for another.

Otherworking is not a type of resting but a malformed way to rest. It is not the way Jesus rested, and it isn't the way that Jesus calls and commands us to rest. Like laziness, otherworking is a selfish way to rest. We can love our neighbor with our rest, but we are not doing so when we otherwork. Our spouses and kids may benefit from our spring-cleaning and from a well-organized home, but not at the expense of our free time with them. Our roommates may appreciate that we do the dishes and fix the shower, but not at the expense of us not attending the cookout. We need to fix things, and build tree houses for the kids, and scrub the kitchen tile, and plan for the family vacation, but we have to be careful not to do these things in a way that ignores, excludes, or hurts our neighbor.

Sabbath Keeping and Renewed Resting

It's tough to find rest in our world. Busy streets, crowded stores, and noise are everywhere. Not to mention the many daily and weekly disasters, distractions, and routine disruptions that surround us. Children whining and tugging on our legs put us on edge. We're worried about what our friends will think when we reply "no" to those birthday parties and dinner invites. And just as we're responding, a solicitor knocks on the door. As we're walking to the door, our phone chimes, indicating that we've received an email or a text message. It's tough to find rest—it's tough to even begin winding down.

Add into the mix our nine-to-five jobs and our daily labor. We do a lot, and we work a lot. If you're a junior investor on Wall Street, you're putting in anywhere from seventy to eighty-five hours a week. The medical resident must be putting in something like eighty. The stay-at-home parent is putting in . . . well, who really knows? A parent is never "off the clock," really. It's tough to find rest when disasters, distractions, and everyday disruptions hit us. But it's equally tough, or I should say, it's even more difficult to find rest when we are inundated with "work" demands, responsibilities, and tasks. How can we rest when we are always doing something? It's tough to find time to rest in our busy world, and it's even tougher not to make rest its own work.

Putting the Sabbath in Perspective

What exactly is the Sabbath, and what does it mean to remember or observe it? What does that look like? At its most basic level, the Sabbath is a time or a day to rest. It's about taking a break from our work. It's about stepping back from our daily toil and seeing what we've done—how much we've accomplished and the quality of work we've done. It's about letting God grow what we've done and make it flourish. This isn't just a random or strange act that God commands we observe once a week—it's so much more. It's a practice that taps into and renews an activity that we do every day. That is, if we look closely and think about it, Sabbath keeping is a practice that corrects and renews the way that we rest.

There are many misconceptions not only about the Sabbath (i.e., Sundays in North American democratic society) but about rest in general. We often confuse the Sabbath with other forms of rest, and we often think wrongly of rest in general. As we read in the passages above and others throughout the Bible, it's clear that the Sabbath isn't meant as a day for us to be lazy and sit on the couch all day. We are told in the Gospel of Mark that Jesus was in the synagogue on the Sabbath and that he healed a man with a withered hand (Mark 3:1–6). Jesus wasn't at home sitting on the couch but was out and about. He was "doing good on the Sabbath." He was helping others.

Sleep is probably what most often comes to mind when we think of rest or observing the Sabbath. In fact, it's probably what most of us do on the Sabbath. We can think of no better way to feel refreshed after a long week around the kids or coworkers than spending an entire day—probably for many of us Saturday or Sunday—dozing off while watching football or binge-watching *Grey's Anatomy, New Girl,* or *Downton Abbey.* Getting much-needed "shut-eye" is the rest that we need. That is what we want to do on this day off from work. We go to church, and then we just plop down on the couch and take a nap for a few hours . . . or a day. That's rest, right? That's how we can and should spend our Sabbath, right? That's a good way to spend the Sabbath, isn't it?

Entertainment and recreation are two other legitimate forms of resting that we also often confuse with Sabbath keeping. To be entertained is to be amused by something or someone else. It is almost entirely passive. It means that the one who wants to be entertained wants to do nothing. He wants to have others do something and he wants to be amused by it. Binge-watching *Grey's Anatomy, New Girl,* or *Downton Abbey* would be entertainment. Recreation, in contrast, is more active. Most would say that even though you are active, such as playing kickball in the park, you are not working. Recreation, though often an active affair, is in most people's mind a break from our jobs. When we "recreate," we are playing—we are doing an activity that we enjoy, which presumably is not what we do when we work.

Sleeping, laughing, and playing are good human activities in themselves, and they should be practiced more in our society. With our penchant for workaholism, we could use more sleep. With our anxiety-ridden work, we could afford to laugh and to play a bit more. Be that as it may, these activities are not the kind of rest that God calls, commands, and commissions us to practice. Rather, the kind of rest God wishes for us to practice involves "stepping back" and doing some kind of reflective activity, not mindless enjoyment of something amusing. It also involves putting an end to strenuous physical activities. How can we genuinely rest if we are playing football all day on our day off? That's not going to rest us up; it's going to exhaust us even more. Though playful and at times restful, recreation is just a different kind of labor, and entertainment is just a distraction from true rest. If we're honest with ourselves and attentive to our minds and bodies, we would agree that sleep, entertainment, and recreation do not always or actually bring us the kind of rest that we want and need.

Loving Others with Our Rest

Many of us brought up in the Christian tradition were taught that the spiritual discipline of Sabbath keeping involves being at home with family and being aware of God. For some of us this meant that we ate breakfast together, listened to worship songs before church, went to church, and then took afternoon naps. In the evenings we let our hair down a little bit and tuned in to football and ate pizza. For some it meant reciting the Heidelberg Catechism or discussing the sermon from earlier in the morning.

While there's nothing wrong with spending time with family, sitting still, taking naps, watching football, reciting a catechism, or discussing a sermon, I think we've failed to see something important and vital in our practice of Sabbath keeping. We've reduced this discipline and made it into something that fits what we want or need. It's not simply about stepping back from what we've done and seeing what we've done, reflecting on it, and letting God grow it and make it flourish. It isn't even merely about our rest as individuals. When we look closely and read further in the biblical story, we see that something much greater is going on here. There's a horizontal dimension to this practice that we have overlooked or ignored.

Protestant Reformer John Calvin (1509–1564) carefully rummaged through the Bible and the early church fathers and concluded that there are three general reasons why we are commanded to keep the fourth commandment ("Remember the sabbath day, and keep it holy").[1] His discussion of these reasons shows the real practical import that the weekly discipline of Sabbath keeping has for our lives.

First, we practice Sabbath keeping so that we can meditate on God's kingdom with others. Because we are so busy throughout the week, it's easy for us to forget in the hustle and bustle of our lives that this is God's world, he reigns, and we work for him. He is King, and we are his citizens (Eph. 2:19). We need to be reminded of this weekly, and we need to do so corporately, so that all of us can hear God's story together and encourage one another. This is one reason we gather with the people of God in worship on Sundays. We gather to hear what God did in the past, share with others what God is doing now in our lives, and hope together for what God will one day do. We hear about what God is doing or what's happening on the other side of his kingdom.

Second, we practice Sabbath keeping so that each of us can meditate on God's works personally. We lay aside our work and our concerns to think about God's work in our own lives. After hearing the good news of God's sovereignty through the biblical story of creation, fall, redemption, and consummation, we take time to think about these movements and actions in our own lives. The Sabbath carves out time for us to think, wonder, and discern: Where is God working in my life? What is he doing? Where am I resisting or rebelling? How can I give this problem, concern, desire, or gift to him? Where can I deliberately open up to his redemption and renewing in my life? Where is he setting up his throne in my life? Where is Jesus calling me to follow him? In what things is the Holy Spirit inviting me to change?

These first two reasons for Sabbath keeping probably make sense to any of us who grew up in a Christian home or remember Sunday school catechism lessons. But the third one might surprise us a little. We most likely forgot about this one. Or our parents and Sunday school teachers didn't really emphasize it. In his presentation of it, Calvin takes his cues from passages such as these:

> But the seventh day is a sabbath to the LORD your God; you shall not do any work—you, or your son or your daughter, or your male or female slave, or your ox or your donkey, or any of your livestock, or the resident alien in your towns, so that your male and female slave may rest as well as you. (Deut. 5:14)

> Six days you shall do your work, but on the seventh day you shall rest, so that your ox and your donkey may have relief, and your homeborn slave and the resident alien may be refreshed. (Exod. 23:12)

The third reason we practice the Sabbath is to ensure that we don't oppress those who work for us. We give others a day off.

We take a day off to afford others under our authority to have respite from their toil. We relieve them of their duties or responsibilities. We take a day off so that they can have a day off, too. This goes for anyone who labors and puts in effort for us. If we have subordinates of any kind, we don't make them work. Now I would expect that most of us don't have maids, gardeners, or pool boys. We may, however, have people who are under our care and authority. For example, some of us have children who do chores. Others have dog walkers. At church we have volunteers. Are they getting a day off from all labor and effort? Ideally, for any of those under our care or authority, keeping the Sabbath would lead us to make it a day for them to worship and fellowship with us.

At the heart of Sabbath keeping is the idea that our bums and our rest belong to God. They are not our own—we are not our own (1 Cor. 6:19–20). Consequently, what we do with our bums and rest matters to God. As he seems to tell us, our rest as well as our working, eating, talking, socializing, thinking, and owning should be done in ways that honor him and help our neighbor. He created us to rest, and he redeemed our rest from our selfish tendencies. Now our rest needs to be renewed in our concrete, everyday practice of it. Laziness and otherworking are not the ways that God invites us to rest. These malformed ways of resting do not give us the rest that we need, and they do not lift up and love our neighbor or heal and harmonize our world in the way God seems to desire. Resting should mean that our neighbor will rest and that we rest with our neighbor. It's about worshiping and fellowshiping with her, not just working with her.

This notion probably rubs you the wrong way. And it should. Of all things, rest seems like the most personal and private affair, doesn't it? "How I rest and what I do to rest is up to me! Isn't rest all about me getting refreshed to go back into the world on Monday?" To suggest that in our rest we ought to consider others is just preposterous! "Rest is rest *for me.*" Rest is personal, that's for sure. Rest is rest for you. You need rest. When you rest, it is you who is resting. Yet the kind of rest that God calls each and every one of us to observe isn't private. It isn't found in isolation. It isn't granted in selfishness. It's not a time for us to sit on the couch with our hands folded, nor is it a day for us to be on our knees with our heads bowed. This behavior confuses the Sabbath with other forms of rest. The Sabbath isn't about sleeping, being amused, or playing all day. Our rest ought to be personal but not private.

The picture the Bible paints for us is that to find true rest, which presumably is the kind of rest that God calls, commands, and commissions us to practice, we must rest in God and we must do so with others as we fellowship with them on our day of rest. Apparently there is something about being with others and worshiping and fellowshiping with them that fosters true rest. Our rest is found in God as we remember his works in the world and in our lives. Coupled with this, rest is found in letting others take time off from their work to do the same. On the one day that God has consecrated for us to experience true rest, he commands us not only to relieve our neighbor of her tasks and responsibilities but to gather and fellowship with her. What a counterintuitive idea and a countercultural practice! Being with our neighbor is not in conflict with our rest, nor is it ancillary to rest. Rather, it's central.

In the hustle and bustle of our lives and in setting up shop in the condition of our selfishness, we have lost control of our resting. We quickly and easily turn our rest time into "me time." We make it a time for indulgences and relaxing pleasures. We isolate ourselves to get away from the problems and annoyances of the world. We want escape undisturbed from our busy world and our bothersome neighbors. When we do this, our rest becomes a time that we don't want to share with others. It becomes a time when we're most interested in getting away from others and treating ourselves. We're interested in making ourselves happy. But according to the Bible, this is not how true or genuine rest is found. If we take God's word for it, the refreshment and rejuvenation that we are seeking will not be found in our indulgences that come from being alone.

We could use revitalization in our rest. We could use some regulation in and with our rest. True resting habits and practices need to be resuscitated in our lives. We need to control our resting and our resting patterns. We work hard, but we need to chill out hard, too. And we need to chill out in the right way—a way that will bring us true rest and enable us to love our neighbor through it. The discipline of Sabbath keeping helps us do this.

Sabbath keeping is a practice that remedies and renews our selfish resting. The Sabbath introduces a weekly rhythm into our busy lives that puts our neighbor front and center. It leads us to give space to our neighbor so that she can have a day to attend to herself, while we attend to ourselves. It not only gives her and us this time for personal attention; it also gives both of us time to worship and fellowship with one another. Depending on the situation and the industry, our practice of Sabbath keeping can also allow others to rest even if they don't work for us. When we discipline ourselves to not work, we invite our neighbor to do the same. When she sees that we carve out time and space in our lives to rejuvenate ourselves so that we can return to our work the following day with renewed energy, inspiration, mission, and excellence, we invite our neighbor to do the same. It also gives us time to talk and fellowship with her in ways that we probably aren't able to do at work.

The Sabbath was made for us (Mark 2:27), yet I think we can say with proper confidence that it ought to be practiced just as much for the well-being of our neighbor as for our own rest. We need a break from our work, which is why God commands us to take one. We need to think about what we've made. We need to appreciate and delight in it. We need some time to recharge so that we can continue working to the best of our abilities. Reflection on our jobs can help us improve our work and our work environment with our coworkers and fellow contributors to society. Just as having a day off can bring us back to engaging our craft with renewed energy and mission, reflecting on our work and our work environment for a day can help us see where God is at work in our lives and where we can be more responsive. Instead of just going through the motions of our job, oblivious to where God is at work, a Sabbath reflection can help us prepare our head, heart, and hands for the week.

In a world where people treat their day off or the weekend as an extended splash of self-centered indulgences in which they forget, ignore, neglect, and even avoid their neighbor to do what they want to do, the weekly practice of Sabbath keeping can be an act of love toward our neighbor. It leads us to discipline our rest so that we can liberate our neighbor from work expectations and demands and possibly worship and fellowship with her. But even if she doesn't go to our church, there are other neighbors at church with whom we can worship and fellowship. Weekly, though, the Sabbath reminds us of our need to care for our neighbor and chat with her, and it gives us the opportunity to love our neighbor through simple deeds like resting. Our rest, if done as God commanded, can liberate, heal, and benefit our neighbor, which is why God has even commanded it.

We can and should love our neighbor with our rest. All we have to do is make small adjustments to our habits and practices of resting, such as being consistent about our practice of Sabbath keeping. By making the practice of Sabbath keeping a part of our weekly rhythm, we can bring health and healing to our neighbor's life. Maybe all that does it is a word of encouragement at church that we wouldn't be able to give at that moment if we didn't go. Maybe it's the relief of not seeing a work email from us so she doesn't have to think about work on her day off. Maybe it's the meal we buy for her after church and before we head to the game with her. If we truly want to love our neighbor as ourselves, we need to change how we rest and how we rest with our neighbor. We need to change what we do when we rest, and we need to invite our neighbor to rest as well. We need to love her with our rest as much as our heads, hands, and pockets.

Side Steps: Sabbath Keeping

Prayer

Infinite Father, you rest. After creating and finishing a finite world, you stood back from it, appreciated it, and delighted in it. May we rely on your strength and power to work and may we learn to rest and delight as you do. Jesus, teach us to do good on the Sabbath and heal our neighbor in the itty-bitty ways that we can. Help us to find

*rest in our fellowship with our neighbor in you. Holy Spirit, prompt
us to slow down at the end of the week and take time to assess how
we are treating our neighbor. Convict us of our insensitivities and
move us to be more sensitive to our neighbor's needs. In Jesus's name
we pray. Amen.*

Simple Steps to Practice Sabbath Keeping

- A simple way to practice Sabbath keeping is to turn off notifications on your phone for the weekend. Don't check your email until Monday morning when you are back at your job. I know this sounds crazy, but maybe even turn off your phone for a day. Most likely, the world will still be there tomorrow, and not much will have changed.

- When you stop seeing church as a place to get filled and you see it as people doing life together, getting up on Sunday morning becomes all the more important. You want to practice Sabbath keeping? Go to church! Worship and fellowship. Be encouraged and edify others.

- Remember the past, think about the present, and anticipate the future. This is something I learned from a Roman "politician" and philosopher named Lucius Annaeus Seneca.[2] It can be adapted and used as a helpful guide for reflecting on God's kingdom, our work, and how we can benefit others on the Sabbath.

- Ask yourself the following questions when you rest.

  » Past: Where has God been in my life? Did God comfort me when I was suffering? Did God give me peace when I was unsure of my future? Was I overjoyed by what God did when I trusted in him? What has my neighbor given to me this week? Where has my neighbor helped me? How have family, friends, acquaintances, and strangers helped me at one time or another? For what should I be grateful? Who should I have thanked? What should I have done?

» Present: Where is God working in my life right now? Is what I'm doing right now in line with God's kingdom? In what areas of my life am I not letting him take the reins? Where do I need to give up control? Where is he in my work? To what end is my work glorifying him and serving my neighbor? Where is my neighbor currently helping me? How are family, friends, acquaintances, and strangers helping me?

» Future: Where could I glorify and honor God in my life? Where could I serve and love my neighbor? What can I do better this week? How can I help and heal my neighbor this week? How can I avoid bringing her undue adversity, pain, or suffering? How can I love her? How can I express my gratitude or appreciate her this upcoming week?

+ + + + + + + + + +
# NINE
+ + + + + + + + + +

WHO'S AFRAID OF LOVE?

EVERYDAY DISCIPLINE FOR THE LIFE OF THE WORLD

A Plumper Public

In this little book, I have tried to show that there is a horizontal dimension to spiritual disciplines, which we tend to overlook, ignore, or avoid. I have suggested that looking at spiritual disciplines from the side shows us how these practices capitalize on the everyday activities that we already do and remedy and renew the malformed ways that we perform these daily deeds. When we step back and look at the big picture, we see that spiritual disciplines impact more than simply our individual habits and practices. We are whole persons who are interconnected with so many other people and things, so as these disciplines correct the habits and practices of our minds and bodies, they inevitably impact the livelihoods of others.

Along with impacting individual people and their lifestyles, our changed behavior influences the dynamics of the community of which both of us are a part. Changing our routines and daily deeds

FIGURE 9.1

cultivates a certain kind of social mind-set and an awareness of shared spaces with others. A change in our habits and practices as lovers, friends, parents, neighbors, citizens, and colleagues leads to a change in shared spaces where we take up these roles, such as our home, workspace, restaurants, parks, and schools (see fig. 9.1). When we step back and look at the disciplines from this perspective, we see them as a way of living. When we do this, we can fully register the impact they have in and on our world. First, we'll see how they *reform malformed habits* and practices for us as individuals. Second, we'll notice how they *reconcile broken relationships* that we have with family, friends, strangers, and enemies. Third, we can consider how these disciplines *renew distorted cultural practices* in society. We could also explore how they *restore corrupt institutions*.

Changed behavior not only affects other people; it changes the places where people live. Our habits, practices, and overall lifestyle impact many aspects of our social environment. For this reason we should consider spiritual disciplines as cultural practices *renovata*—renewed cultural practices. They change the way we—society—live, think, eat, talk, own, socialize, work, and rest. Because we have a narrow view of the "public," many of us don't see these wider implications of the spiritual disciplines. When we talk about "public life," many of us simply mean life outside our home and around other people—while life inside our home is our "private life." Whatever is public is what can be seen or heard by others outside the four walls that we call "home."

So when Christians talk about "faith and public life," we usually mean this in terms of how to vote, what to say when we're asked about or confronted with a moral or political issue, or how to act when things get heated at school or at work. We mean how we should conduct ourselves in front of colleagues, newscasters, fans, or spectators. Naturally, this leads us to think that our witness to the world primarily or exclusively depends on how we vote on a controversial issue, what we say after a game (e.g., "I want to thank my Lord and Savior Jesus Christ"), what social movement we get behind and tag on social media, or what political party we support. What can be seen and heard by others is important. And how we conduct ourselves in front of a camera is also worth considering. But this puny view of the public captures only a tiny portion of how our faith informs "public life."

We need a richer understanding of shared spaces. We need a plumper view of the public, a thicker or chunkier one that understands how our beliefs and practices affect those around us. As Christians, we need to see the intricate and detailed ways that our spiritual formation impacts our interpersonal life in all sorts of shared spaces—including the home. We eat in commissaries or cafeterias. We think in boardrooms and classrooms. We rest in pods or on benches. We help on company service or volunteer days. We socialize at happy hour or at our child's dance class. What if we did these things differently? Every day we do things in culture and society that are shaped by others, and every day we have the opportunity to shape culture and society and to help others by changing the way we do these things.

Changed personal practices have professional and political import. A change in the way we do basic everyday activities not only changes us and those around us; it changes some pretty important procedures and practices in society.

Through the reformation of our habits and behavior comes the transformation of our shared world with our neighbor. Through the regeneration of our daily living comes the renewal and revitalization of our neighbor's livelihood. Through the pursuit of holiness comes harmonious and healthy living in our neighborhoods. Our personal holiness is inseparable from interpersonal harmony (Gal. 5:14). Our acts of worship are inseparable from acts of love.

By practicing these disciplines, we are not detaching ourselves from human life and the activities of human life. We don't stop doing everyday activities. We still talk, eat, rest, own, and so forth. We just change when and how we do these things. What if our witness to the world isn't how we vote on a controversial issue, what we say after a game, or the social movement or political party we support? What if our greatest and most unique witness to the world is found in doing everyday activities alongside others in society—but doing them differently? What if living for others in the little things is our greatest witness? What if that is how we really tell people about Jesus and live out his kingdom? What if that is how we can change the world and love our neighbor as ourselves?

If we want to change people, if we want to "win" souls for Christ, if we want to bring health, healing, and harmony to the world, we need to do very basic but nonetheless important things differently. We need to do the same mundane, ordinary things that we've been doing every day but do them differently. We need to change the way we eat, rest, think, work, talk, live, and socialize. We need to practice these things differently in and with our communities. If we want to love others as ourselves, we can do so in and through the little things—things that everyone else does selfishly but that we do sacrificially.

Disciplining Liturgy?

Spiritual disciplines play a central part in our sanctification as believers and in God's renewal of all things. When seen from the side, spiritual disciplines are concrete and essential ways that God renews and revitalizes our lives and our life in society with others. God changes you and me here and now through what we do here and now. And the most basic and forceful way this happens is through the little things we do every day—our daily deeds.

We cannot mistake our practice of spiritual disciplines for "works righteousness" though. We do not save ourselves through spiritual disciplines, nor do we save the world through them. Jesus is the one who saves us and saves the world, if he so chooses. He is the one with the authority and the power to recover, redeem, regenerate, reprove, and resurrect this world. These things we cannot do. But he does invite us to help him remedy what is wrong and repair what has been broken. He redeems, but he invites us to help

him repair. When seen from the side, spiritual disciplines are creative and essential practices for our work as agents of repair who
are on a mission with God to fix the breach in the created order
(Isa. 58:12). They are unique ways to concretely love our neighbor
and bring life to the world. As they remedy our broken lives, they
reconcile damaged relationships, renew distorted cultural practices, and restore corrupt institutions. They are healthy for us,
and they bring healing and harmony to our shared life together in
this world.

What does all of this mean for Sunday morning worship though?
Is Sunday morning worship not an act of love in some mysterious or
mystical way? Does God not renew us then and there? What about
ecclesiastical or liturgical practices? Does the Eucharist or confession
not form us? What's the relationship between the church's liturgical
practices and spiritual disciplines? A helpful way to answer these
questions may be to clarify what we mean by "church." In my tradition (Reformed), we distinguish between the *church as institution* and
the *church as organism*. The basic idea here is that the institution of
the church meets on Sunday to worship and fellowship together,
while the organism of the church is sent out into the world during
the week. This distinction can help us think about the relationship between liturgical practices and spiritual disciplines. There
are mental and physical, intellectual and moral practices that we
learn in and through the church as an institution, and then there
are similar practices that we do as the church as an organism. I think
of it in the following way.

Liturgy and worship in the institutional church give us a vision
for life (*visio vitae*). They help us see the bigger picture of God's
story of creation, fall, and redemption, and they demonstrate how
life together is to be experienced and conducted in this new life. In
this dramatic schema, liturgical practices are communal practices
that help us see, imagine, and move in the world.[1] They provide a

general rhythm to our year and structure to our lifestyle. Through the liturgy, we learn the importance of greeting others, being invited by God to worship, confessing our sins, hearing that we've been forgiven, passing the peace to others, hearing truth from the Lord, affirming our beliefs as a community, interceding for others in prayer, giving to God through the offering, giving thanks to God for what he's done, and being sent forth to love and serve the world.

Spiritual disciplines do something different. They are a specific way of life (*via vitae*) that witnesses to the vision for life we learn in and through the institutional church. They are the way that we live out this vision concretely, correctly, and consistently every day. To put it succinctly, the liturgy gives us a picture for how we should think, eat, socialize, talk, work, and rest in the way of Jesus, and spiritual disciplines help us live out these practices every day and everywhere. The formative practices of the institutional church grip our desires, our perception, and our action in a general way, which is vital for Christian life. But we also need hands-on training to change the way we specifically and frequently think, eat, socialize, talk, work, and rest. We need to be reformed daily, not just weekly.

Church is not hands-on training. We don't confess, sing hymns, hear a sermon, or take the body and blood of Christ in the Eucharist in order to change the way that we own, think, eat, socialize, talk, work, and rest. We don't go to church to have these habits and practices changed then and there—church isn't a workshop. If it were, then as experience teaches us regarding habits, particularly that they die hard, we would have to engage in these liturgical practices much more often than once a week if we were to actually change them. We would have to go to church every day. However—though formal worship or Sunday school isn't a workshop for improving our behavior—our homes, restaurant, parties, and workplaces can be "portable shops" for us to work on such activities.

If we want to change the way we own, think, eat, socialize, talk, work, and rest, we need to actually practice owning, thinking, eating, socializing, talking, working, and resting differently—not merely talking about reforming them or getting motivated to reform them through praise and worship, challenging sermons, vacation Bible school, or the Eucharist. Because we are made up of habits, we need a specific, sustained change of habits. We need to do these activities differently every day in order to change how we do them.

But we shouldn't see any opposition or dualism between spiritual disciplines and liturgical practices. It is not either/or but rather both/and. Spiritual disciplines don't replace liturgical practices; they supplement them. Both are necessary for Christian discipleship. Liturgical practices push us into spiritual disciplines, and spiritual disciplines consummate in the liturgy. Liturgy shows us how we ought to organize our lives, and spiritual disciplines help us conduct our lives in accordance with this organization. In liturgical practices, we are given a glimpse of how it's supposed to be, and in spiritual disciplines we graft this into our everyday lives. Both are an essential part of God's sanctifying program to renew and reform culture and society. Both are one movement in loving our neighbor. Both are necessary for following Jesus. The Christian life is a consistent and integrated life. It is one in which piety is inseparable from public justice, spirituality is inseparable from ethics, devotion is inseparable from deeds, worship is inseparable from fellowship, and evangelism is inseparable from discipleship.

Working for the Common Good

Spiritual disciplines are an extension of the way of life envisioned by and lived in the church. They embody this vision, but we won't really grasp how impactful they are if we don't have a plumper view of the public. When we see how these disciplines affect the public—that

is, the people around us—we can see that these disciplines really
do benefit the public. In recent years, we Christians have started to
talk more and more about vocation, work, and the common good.
We talk about the work we are called to, the importance of excel-
ling at work for God's glory, and how to work in a way that helps
others through our good work. This is a good conversation for us
to have. Perhaps the day when the Christian could be accused by
such remarks as those of French philosopher Jean-Jacques Rousseau
(1712–1778) is long gone:

> Christianity is a completely spiritual religion, concerned exclusively
> with things heavenly. The homeland of the Christian is not of this
> world. He does his duty, it is true, but he does it with a profound
> indifference toward the success or failure of his efforts. So long as he
> has nothing to reproach himself for, it matters little to him whether
> anything is going well or poorly down here. If the state is flourish-
> ing, he hardly dares to enjoy the public felicity, for fear of becoming
> puffed up with his country's glory. If the state is in decline, he blesses
> the hand of God that weighs heavily on his people.[2]

Yet this conversation, especially our discussion of the common
good, tends to be a bit unwieldy and abstract. What exactly is the
common good, and what does it look like to pursue the common
good?

By "common good" most Christians nowadays have in mind the
basic human rights and resources due a human being: clean water,
a roof over one's head, and freedom from any kind of violence, oppression, slavery, or torture. These are common goods. Everyone
should have clean and sustainable resources, the basic necessities
of life, and freedom. They are due to all, and all share responsibility for helping everyone obtain them. So seeking the common
good typically means that we dig wells in some distant village, or
build houses in third world countries, or free adolescents from

sex-trafficking rings, or perhaps get involved in another kind of social justice movement.

These are definitely important and valuable rights and resources for all human beings, and we should pursue them and fight for others who do not have them. But I wonder if these are the only common goods. Is this the only thing we should fight for in our pursuit of public justice? Is this primarily what we should seek as we work for the common good?

Our discussion of the horizontal dimension of spiritual disciplines can have valuable bearing on these conversations, but only if we broaden our horizons of the "common good" as I've suggested we do with our notion of the "public" and "work" (as discussed in chapter 7).

When you really think about it, working for the common good and pursuing public justice are matters of our daily lives and something we can practice in our daily activities. We can pursue public justice anywhere. As we've already discussed, our common practices affect those around us every day in positive or negative ways. Disrupting and destroying community are matters of public justice. Hurting, harming, oppressing, and ostracizing our neighbor through seemingly innocent and innocuous acts affect the common good. In other words, selfish living is a matter of the common good and public justice.

Running water, freedom to take a walk, and a warm blanket are goods important for all to share in common. So is love. So is sacrifice. And so are the little things that we bestow on our neighbor through our love and sacrifice. Making simple changes in our basic, daily activities can express love for our neighbor. This is a common good we should seek. Love isn't all that common. At least not the kind of love that Jesus calls his disciples to. This kind of love is uncommon. Many people in this world would be willing to die for another person. Because they are kind and caring, they would be willing even to die for those they don't know. They would sacrifice their lives to save another. This is truly an amazing act, but Jesus doesn't call us to simply die for others. He calls us to live for him and to love others. To die for someone is difficult or unimaginable. But to live for someone, well, that is something else. That kind of love is rare, uncommon.

What I am trying to say is that we cannot underestimate the power of simply being loving people who live lives of love. We cannot overlook the value of being people who sacrifice in the littlest of things so that our neighbor can have a more comfortable and peaceful livelihood. We cannot diminish the value and necessity of simply being sensitive to what those around us expect and need. These are truly common goods. These are goods from which everyone can benefit. To change the little things we do so even these things can heal and love our neighbor—that is how we *all* can seek the common good—not just those who have the time, energy, skill, and insight to dig wells, build homes, and rescue victims of violence and oppression.

Our idea of and vision for the "common good" would be more substantive, wieldy, and concrete if we were to see it through the lens of spiritual disciplines, as seen from the side. Conversely, our understanding of spiritual disciplines and our motivation to practice them would be expanded and enriched if we were to look at their broad implications, particularly how they benefit the public and contribute to the common good.

Our calling is first and foremost to live in a particular way. This call is tied to the lifestyle featured and welcomed in these practices that we call "spiritual disciplines." These basic, daily activities that we can practice anew are "good" for the world. They bring life to the world. And the world can do them with us and benefit from them. Doing these disciplines is pursuing public justice and working toward the common good. That is why we should practice them

in our homes and, when possible, at our businesses, schools, and
neighborhood gatherings to varying degrees. If we really want to
seek the common good, if we really want to love our neighbors as
ourselves, if we really want to worship God with all our lives, if we
really want to bring all things under our Savior's rule, we need to
change the way we do our daily deeds.

We seek the common good, love our neighbor, and worship God
when we don't spend lavishly or squander our earnings and possessions, when we aren't self-absorbed or thinking maliciously of others,
when we aren't greedy eaters and monopolizers of food, when we
don't intrude on our neighbor or avoid her, when we aren't loquacious or maligning to others, when don't neglect others or compete
with them at work, and when we're not lazy and don't ignore others
on our rest day. Let's stop being selfish and start sacrificing. Let's
love our neighbor with our heads and thoughts, bellies and urges,
tongues and words, shadows and presences, pockets and possessions,
hands and work, and bums and rest. Let's practice simplicity, meditation, fasting and feasting, solitude, silence, service, and Sabbath
keeping. And let's do this at church, home, work, and everywhere
we find ourselves.

ACKNOWLEDGMENTS

When I think about the debt I owe to the people and communities of which I've been a part, and the gratitude I ought to express to them daily but have failed to do for years, it makes me shudder. So many friends, family members, and strangers have shaped me as a person and accordingly influenced this little book. Perhaps putting their names on paper will be a token of my appreciation. For now.

Thanks to my parents for bringing me into this world and raising me up in the faith and in the knowledge of God. Thanks to my brothers, Chad and Brad, for putting up with me for all these years and letting me win a few b-ball games. Love you guys. Thanks to my friend Nick Barrett, who continues to inspire, edify, reorient, and pull the curtain back on me. If there is a sliver of humanity on these pages, I owe it to Gideon Strauss, who continues to show me what it looks like to be a caring, loving, empowering, and integrated human being. And I wouldn't have been able to do this without my good friends Christopher Romine and Jean Carlos Arce.

Truth is the greatest friend, but what is truth apart from friends, especially when those who have helped you see the truth are your friends? It's a joy to call Rich Mouw and Jamie Smith, my two mentors and PhD supervisors, friends. Rich, I'm grateful for your guidance and hospitality over these years. You continue to model wisdom, discernment, and generosity to me in reading, thinking, writing, and living. Jamie, your insight, kindness, edification, and collegiality from day one have mesmerized and deeply moved me. I look forward to many more years of cocktails on the porch with you and Deanna.

Thanks to my friends Kent Dunnington and Rebecca DeYoung, too. Kent, your enthusiasm, kind criticisms, and accountability were the spark. Thanks for midwifing this book. Rebecca, thanks for your encouragement, wisdom, and tranquility. Our talks give me hope for the future of Christian teaching and being philosophers. Many thanks to Kevin Timpe and the rest of the Intellectual Humility seminar a number of years ago for putting up with me and giving helpful feedback on some of these ideas, especially Kevin and his wife, Allison, Craig Boyd, and James Van Slyke.

I would also like to thank others along the way who made this possible: Grant Goble, Joel Albritton, Veli-Matti Kärkkäinen, Nancey Murphy, Cory Willson, my NYC salon crew (Zach Terrell, Meaghan Ritchey, Scott Calgaro, Joe Kickasola, Alissa Wilkinson, Kevin Gosa, and Drew Dernavich), Ron and Linda Morris, Barb and Ralph Romine Green, Bill and Beverly Romine, Adam and Katie Jackley, Brian and Melinda Wright, Matt Lowe, Devyn Miska, Grant Lowe, Derek Halvorson, Kris Thomas, Joey and Lauren Bastelli, Julie Hamilton, Billy Daniel, Harris Bechtol (to whom I'm eternally grateful for introducing me to Kierkegaard after German class one California evening), and Jim Flynn and Phil Miller, my colleagues at Caldwell University.

I'm stoked to have new friends at Brazos Press and Baker Publishing Group. You all are a pleasant, passionate, and patient group. I look forward to our future together. Thanks especially to Eric Salo and my friend and editor, Bob Hosack. I thoroughly enjoy our time together, Bob, and I look forward to many more dinners with you and Lisa. Your kindness is one of a kind.

The home is a profound and mysterious exercise in city living, and I have the best of neighbors. Elliott, my dear, your questions, hugs, and insatiable appetite for snacks bring me so much joy and cheer. I'm grateful that even though I was preoccupied while writing this book, and at times entirely absent, you made it clear to me that my love for you had not disappeared. Thank you for showing me what it means to have faith like a child. Miles, thanks for not having the words yet to impugn my concentration or consistency as your play pal and best friend. Every day I simultaneously wish I could be interrupted more by you and never have to be interrupted when I'm with you. Your smile and mischievous ways are the stuff of fun and peace. I love you and your sister very, very deeply and earnestly.

Andrea, my partner in crime and law, your love ever so works on me. Thank you for taking care of us. Thank you for sharing your things with us. Thank you for being mindful of us. Thank you for dining with us and giving to us, even when it was your last bite. Thank you for talking to us and wanting to hear from us. Thank you for working with and for us—around the clock. And thank you for making your rest (or the lack thereof!) a means for refreshing us. To you this book is dedicated. I love and appreciate you.

NOTES

Introduction

1. E.g., Barbara Fredrickson, *Positivity: Top-Notch Research Reveals the Upward Spiral That Will Change Your Life* (New York: Harmony, 2009).

2. "Dark Night of the Soul" is the title to a poem written by Catholic mystic St. John of the Cross (1542–1591). The poem, along with a helpful introduction to the life and work of St. John of the Cross, can be found in *The Collected Works of St. John of the Cross*, trans. Kieran Kavanaugh, OCD, and Otilio Rodriguez, OCD (Washington, DC: Institute of Carmelite Studies, 1991).

3. For a positive discussion of the emotions in the Christian's life, see Robert C. Roberts, *Spiritual Emotions: A Psychology of Christian Virtues* (Grand Rapids: Eerdmans, 2007).

4. Consider expectation in terms of the contemporary philosopher Charles Taylor's discussion of "social imaginaries." See his *Modern Social Imaginaries* (Durham, NC: Duke University Press, 2004).

5. I am reminded of Søren Kierkegaard's (1813–1855) belief that, while good news, the gospel is paradoxical in such a way that it is always offensive to us. Keeping this offensive character is essential to the gospel: "If the discourse is to be about the essentially Christian, it must continually hold open the possibility of offense, but then it can never reach the point of *directly* recommending Christianity. . . . Whatever needs the approval of people promptly makes itself palatable to them, but Christianity is so sure of itself and knows with such earnestness and rigor that it is people who need it that for this very reason it does not recommend itself directly but first startles people—just as Christ recommended himself to the apostles by predicting in advance that for his sake they would be hated—yes, that someone who put them to death would think he was doing God a service. . . . If Christianity is to be preached out of the enchantment of illusion and deformed transmogrification . . . ,

then first of all the possibility of offense must be thoroughly preached back to life again." Søren Kierkegaard, *Works of Love*, trans. Howard V. Hong and Edna H. Hong (Princeton: Princeton University Press, 1995), 198–200 (emphasis original).

6. Richard J. Foster, *Celebration of Discipline: The Path to Spiritual Growth*, 3rd ed. (1978; San Francisco: HarperSanFrancisco, 1998).

Chapter 1: Spiritual Disciplines and the Way of Love

1. John Cassian, *The Institutes*, trans. Boniface Ramsey (Mahwah, NJ: Paulist Press, 2000).

2. Even the desert monk—a hermit or anchorite—doesn't ensconce himself to get away from the world; he's actually throwing himself into fellowship with a certain kind of community in this world—those who have gone before him and other creatures around him. He goes to his cell or cave not to conceal himself but to commune and change the way he lives. He, too, seeks to discipline his daily deeds. Cf. Thomas Merton, *Thoughts in Solitude* (New York: Farrar, Straus & Giroux, 1999).

3. Ancient Christians such as Cassian saw the monastic life as the most consistent and integrated life that a Christian could live. Two readable accounts of this are Hans Urs von Balthasar, "Philosophy, Christianity, Monasticism," in *Spouse of the Word: Explorations in Theology*, vol. 2 (San Francisco: Ignatius Press, 1991), 333–72; and Jean Leclercq, *The Love of Learning and the Desire for God*, trans. Catherine Mishrahi (New York: Fordham University Press, 1982).

4. Klaas Schilder, *Christ and Culture*, trans. G. van Rongen and W. Helder (Winnipeg: Premier, 1979), 24 (reference is to section number).

5. Cassian, *Institutes*, 117 (5.1).

6. One of the most rewarding books I've read on the Holy Spirit and one that articulates this line of thinking is Jürgen Moltmann's *The Spirit of Life: A Universal Affirmation* (Minneapolis: Fortress, 1992).

7. Catholic theologian Hans Urs von Balthasar (1905–1988) beautifully weaves this spiritual formation with how we experience Christ. Hans Urs von Balthasar, *Prayer* (San Francisco: Ignatius Press, 1986), 277–93.

8. The ambiguity of Friedrich Nietzsche's (1844–1900) remark is provocative: "Only Christian practice, a *life* such as he lived who *died* on the cross, is Christian" (emphasis mine). Friedrich Nietzsche, *The Antichrist*, §39.

Chapter 2: "What Do You Have That You Did Not Receive?"

1. A humorous and entertaining report of Diogenes's life can be found in James Miller's excellent book *Examined Lives: From Socrates to Nietzsche* (New York: Farrar, Straus & Giroux, 2012).

2. For example, Justin Martyr (100–165), *The First Apology*, chap. 46: "The Word in the World before Christ." A good translation and helpful introduction can be found in Leslie William Barnard's translation in the Ancient Christian Writers series: St. Justin Martyr, *The First and Second Apologies* (Mahwah, NJ: Paulist Press, 1997).

3. Plato, *Apology* 38a.

4. Plato, *Republic* 369a–373e.

5. Hoarding is very different from, say, the hobby of collecting baseball cards. The little boy who goes to the shop every week to pick up another pack isn't hoarding; he's engaging in a hobby. Baseball cards are not to be consumed or used; they are to be collected. Houses, cars, laptops, watches, sneakers, and food, on the other hand, are not meant to be collected.

6. English philosopher John Locke (1632–1704) gives this idea more bite: "If [the products] perished, in [one's] possession, without their due use; if the fruits rotted, or the venison putrified, before he could spend it, he offended against the common law of nature, and was liable to be punished; he invaded his neighbor's share, for he had no *right, farther than his use* called for any of them, and they might serve to afford him conveniences of life" (*Second Treatise on Government*, chap. 5, sec. 37, emphasis original).

7. Thomas Aquinas, *The Three Greatest Prayers: Commentaries on the Lord's Prayer, the Hail Mary, and the Apostle's Creed* (Manchester, NH: Sophia Institute Press, 1990).

8. "Love . . . is a revolution from the ground up. The more profound the revolution, the more completely the distinction 'mine and yours' disappears, and the more perfect is the love." Søren Kierkegaard, *Works of Love*, trans. Howard V. Hong and Edna H. Hong (Princeton: Princeton University Press, 1995), 266.

9. Contemporary poet and writer Wendell Berry puts it like this: "The human economy, if it is to be a good economy, must fit harmoniously within and must correspond to the Great Economy; in certain important ways, it must be an analogue of the Great Economy." "Two Economies," in *The Art of the Commonplace: The Agrarian Essays of Wendell Berry*, ed. Norman Wirzba (Washington, DC: Counterpoint, 2002), 223. Matthew C. Halteman articulates some of these concerns in his *Compassionate Eating as Care of Creation* (Washington, DC: Humane Society of the United States), especially 10.

Chapter 3: Directions for Ruling the Mind

1. This is a verse from "voices to voices, lip to lip." It can be found in the recently released volume E. E. Cummings, *Complete Poems, 1904–1962*, ed. George James Firmage (New York: Liveright, 2016).

2. Strictly speaking, malice isn't essentially a thought; it's a disposition of the will. It's wishing, willing, or wanting something bad to befall someone, which is different from thinking about something bad happening to someone. Malice can take hold of our thinking, and our thinking can become an extension of malicious willing. An accessible and clearly written discussion of disposition can be found in Philip E. Dow, *Virtuous Minds: Intellectual Character Development* (Downers Grove, IL: InterVarsity, 2013). A more detailed but still very clear and insightful discussion can be found in Robert C. Roberts and W. Jay Wood, *Intellectual Virtues: An Essay in Regulative Epistemology* (New York: Oxford University Press, 2007).

3. On this point, see Anthony J. Steinbock, *Moral Emotions: Reclaiming the Evidence of the Heart* (Evanston, IL: Northwestern University Press, 2014), 11–17.

4. A helpful guide by a top-notch scholar is John Cottinham's *How to Read Descartes* (London: Granta Books, 2009).

5. John Cassian, *Conferences*, trans. Boniface Ramsey (Mahwah, NJ: Paulist Press, 1997), "Ninth Conference: On Prayer, Part 1" and "Tenth Conference: On Prayer, Part 2," 323–93.

6. We are already "in touch with the world" before we're aware of it, as French philosopher Maurice Merleau-Ponty (1908–1961) rightly noted. "The world is there before any possible analysis" of ours. *Phenomenology of Perception*, trans. Colin Smith (London: Routledge & Kegan Paul, 1962), vii–xxi.

7. "Attention animated by desire is the whole foundation of religious practices." Simone Weil, *Waiting for God*, trans. Emma Craufurd (New York: HarperPerennial, 2009), 129.

8. Cf. Peter Ochs, "Morning Prayer as Redemptive Thinking," in *Liturgy, Time, and the Politics of Redemption*, ed. Randi Rashkover and C. C. Pecknold (Grand Rapids: Eerdmans, 2006), 50–90.

Chapter 4: This Is My Tummy, Which I Will Curb for You

1. John Climacus offers a powerful image of the nature of gluttony: "Gluttony answers us: 'Why are you complaining, you who are my servants? How is it that you are trying to get away from me? Nature has bound me to you. The door for me is what food actually is, its character and quality. The reason for my being insatiable is habit. Unbroken habit, dullness of soul, and the failure to remember death are the roots of my passion. And how is it that you are looking for the names of my offspring? For if I were to count them, their number would be greater than the total of the grains of sand.'" John Climacus, *Ladder of Divine Ascent*, trans. Colm Luibheid and Norman Russell (Mahwah, NJ: Paulist Press, 1982), 170 ("Step 14: On Gluttony").

2. Langston Hughes, "Ballad of the Miser," in *The Collected Poems of Langston Hughes*, ed. Arnold Rampersad (New York: Vintage Classics, 1995), 221–22.

3. John Cassian, *The Institutes*, trans. Boniface Ramsey (Mahwah, NJ: Paulist Press, 2000), 133 (5.26).

4. Gregory the Great, *Pastoral Rule*, trans. Henry Davis, SJ (Mahwah, NJ: Newman Press, 1978), 150.

5. Cf. Eric Schlosser, *Fast Food Nation: The Dark Side of the All-American Meal* (New York: Houghton Mifflin, 2001).

6. Norman Wirzba, *Food and Faith: A Theology of Eating* (New York: Cambridge University Press, 2011), 137.

Chapter 5: Time-Out for Adults

1. Christine Smallwood, "Where the Swedes Go to Be (Really) Alone," *New York Times Style Magazine*, May 16, 2016.

2. Henry David Thoreau, "Walden; Or, Life in the Woods," in *Henry David Tho-reau: A Week on the Concord and Merrimack Rivers / Walden; Or, Life in the Woods / The Maine Woods / Cape Cod* (New York: Library of America, 1989), 430–31.

3. We often think of image bearing exclusively in individual terms. But Herman Bavinck (1854–1921) stressed the corporate nature and diversity of the image: "Just as God did not reveal himself all at once at the creation, but continues and expands that revelation from day to day and from age to age, so also the image of God is not a static entity but extends and unfolds itself in the forms of space and time. . . . Only humanity in its entirety—as one complete organism, summed up under a single head, spread out over the whole earth, as prophet proclaiming the truth of God, as priest dedicating itself to God, as ruler controlling the earth and the whole of creation—only it is the fully finished image, the most telling and striking like-ness of God." *Reformed Dogmatics*, ed. John Bolt, trans. John Vriend, vol. 2, *God and Creation* (2004; repr., Grand Rapids: Baker Academic, 2008), 577.

4. This is why it might be salutary to abstain or "fast" from social media too. Cf. Norman Wirzba, *Food and Faith: A Theology of Eating* (New York: Cambridge University Press, 2011), 142.

Chapter 6: Controlling the Chatterbox

1. Roger Hargreaves, *Little Miss Chatterbox* (New York: Price Stern Sloan, 1999), n.p.

2. Jean-Louis Chrétien, "The Wounded Word: The Phenomenology of Prayer," in *Phenomenology and the "Theological Turn": The French Debate* (Bronx, NY: Fordham University Press, 2000), 168.

3. William Shakespeare, *All's Well That Ends Well*, ed. Claire McEachern (New York: Penguin Classics, 2001), line 30.

4. Christine D. Pohl, *Making Room: Recovering Hospitality as a Christian Tradition* (Grand Rapids: Eerdmans, 1999), 13.

Chapter 7: How to Make Friends and Empower People

1. On this distinction, see Hannah Arendt's work *The Human Condition* (Chicago: University of Chicago Press, 1958; 1998), particularly part 4: "Work."

2. Norman Wirzba, *Food and Faith: A Theology of Eating* (New York: Cambridge University Press, 2011), 196.

Chapter 8: Work Hard, Consecrate Hard

1. John Calvin, *Institutes of the Christian Religion*, ed. John T. McNeill, trans. Ford Lewis Battles (Louisville: Westminster John Knox, 1960), 2.8.33.

2. Seneca, "Tranquility of Mind," in *The Stoic Philosophy of Seneca: Essays and Letters*, trans. Moses Hadas (New York: W. W. Norton, 1968), 75–106.

Chapter 9: Who's Afraid of Love?

1. "Part of what identifies the Christian church as a distinct people in history is that it engages in the Christian liturgy" (Nicholas Wolterstorff, "Justice as a Condition of Authentic Liturgy," in *Hearing the Call: Liturgy, Justice, Church, and World*, ed. Mark R. Gornik and Gregory Thompson [Grand Rapids: Eerdmans, 2011], 39–58, here 39). Elsewhere Wolterstorff says, "A rhythmic alternation of work and worship, labor and liturgy, is one of the significant distinguishing features of the Christian's way of being-in-the-world" ("The Tragedy of Liturgy in Protestantism," in *Hearing the Call*, 29–38, here 30).

2. Jean-Jacques Rousseau, *The Social Contract*, trans. Donald A. Cress (Indianapolis: Hackett, 1987), 100 (4.8).

FURTHER READING

While this little book has explored the various ways that spiritual disciplines impact our everyday living in concrete ways, it did not drop out of the sky. So many other great books, thinkers, and writers have formed my perception, imagination, and judgment in these matters. Here are a few key ones:

Bass, Dorothy C., ed. *Practicing Our Faith: A Way of Life for a Searching People*. 1997. San Francisco, CA: Jossey-Bass, 2010. Bass shows how the Christian faith is a way of life and discusses twelve central practices that Christians can do every day.

Crouch, Andy. *Culture Making: Recovering Our Creative Calling*. Downers Grove, IL: InterVarsity, 2008. Crouch discusses and explores the cultural mandate (Gen. 1:28) and our calling as Christians to make cultural artifacts and contribute to society.

DeYoung, Rebecca Konyndyk. *Glittering Vices: A New Look at the Seven Deadly Sins and Their Remedies*. Grand Rapids: Brazos, 2009. DeYoung offers a witty and insightful discussion of the "vice tradition" and a contemporary exploration of some spiritual disciplines as correctives to these vices.

Kenneson, Philip D. *Life on the Vine: Cultivating the Fruit of the Spirit*. Downers Grove, IL: InterVarsity, 1999. This reflection on the "fruits of the Spirit" presented by the apostle Paul in Galatians 5:22–23 but

in the context of contemporary culture and Christian practice is one
of the first books that got me thinking about spirituality and society.

Kierkegaard, Søren. *Works of Love*. Translated by Howard V. Hong and
Edna H. Hong. Princeton: Princeton University Press, 1995. This book
is a complex and provocative discourse on the vast dimensions of love.
Devotional reading par excellence!

Mouw, Richard. *Uncommon Decency: Christian Civility in an Uncivil World*.
Downers Grove, IL: InterVarsity, 1992. Rev. ed. 2010. Mouw presents a
clearly written and engaging study of spirituality and public life through
the lens of civility.

Peterson, Eugene. *A Long Obedience in the Same Direction: Discipleship in
an Instant Society*. 1980. Downers Grove, IL: InterVarsity, 2000. Anything by Peterson is worth gobbling and digesting. This gem brings to
the fore the importance of discipline for obedience and of obedience
for discipleship.

Smith, James K. A. *Desiring the Kingdom: Worship, Worldview, and Cultural
Formation*. Grand Rapids: Baker Academic, 2009. Layered with complex
and subtle theses, this book shows the importance of Christian thinking about habit, how we are formed through the habits and practices of
"cultural liturgies" and institutions, and how the institutional church
and the Christian university are countercultural agents.

———. *Imagining the Kingdom: How Worship Works*. Grand Rapids: Baker
Academic, 2013. A sequel to *Desiring the Kingdom*, this book shows
how habits and practices shape our imagination and perception of the
world. Smith ties this to worship—liturgy, catechesis, and Christian
education—and how it "works" on us.

Willard, Dallas. *The Spirit of the Disciplines: Understanding How God Changes
Lives*. New York: HarperCollins, 1988. A classic. Willard discusses the
importance of the disciplines for personal transformation and as a way
of life for disciples.

Wirzba, Norman. *Food and Faith: A Theology of Eating*. New York: Cambridge University Press, 2011. This profound work deserves much more
attention and discussion. Wirzba sets eating in a broad framework that
discusses soil, gardening, forestation, fisheries, Sabbath, feasting, fasting,
communion, and banqueting in heaven.

INDEX

abnegation, distinct from fasting, 85–86
abstemiousness, distinct from fasting, 84, 85
abstention, distinct from fasting, 84
All's Well That Ends Well (Shakespeare), 125
Aquinas, Thomas, 51–52, 185n7
Aristotle, 65
asceticism, 48
avoidance of others, 96, 99, 108, 109, 127

body and spirit, 23

calling, xiv, 23, 26, 70, 75, 140, 158, 177, 189
Calvin, John, 157, 159, 187n1 (chap. 8)
Cassian, John, xi, 17–19, 83–84, 184n3
cell phone. *See* phone
Chrétien, Jean-Louis, 123, 187n2 (chap. 6)
Christian philosophy of public affairs, xii, xv
church, 83, 86, 88, 99, 138, 141, 156, 168, 174, 178

in Ephesus, 122
history of, xi, 5, 13
as institution and organism, 36, 172–73, 190
liturgy of, 188n1
not hands-on training, 173
parachurch organizations, 54
Protestant, 3, 65
retreats, 108
volunteers, 159
as workshop, 173
worship, 4, 157, 163, 164
youth ministry, 33, 147
commandments, xii, xiv, 24, 25, 26, 31, 69, 70, 157–58
common good, 50, 133, 174–78
competition, 133–35
contest, 134
continence, distinct from fasting, 85
Cummings, E. E., 62, 185n1

daily deeds
disciplining, 19, 20, 21, 23, 25, 55, 126, 184n2

impact on neighbor, 34, 35, 93, 142, 143–44, 178
renewing, xv, 27, 28, 73, 104, 111, 128, 140, 167, 171
Descartes, René, 65–66, 186n4 (chap. 3)
Devil Wears Prada (film), 117
diligence, 131
Diogenes of Sinope, 39–40, 41, 42, 48, 184n1 (chap. 2)
disciple, xi, xiv, xv, 15, 16, 20, 22, 24–26, 29–32, 35, 100, 105, 106, 176
discipleship, xi, 20, 23, 29, 174, 190
discipline, xv, 20, 21–22, 24
distinct from punishment, 22

Elf (film), 116
emotions, in our relationship with God, 3–5
entertainment, distinct from rest, 156, 157

faith and public life, 169
fasting, distinct from other similar practices, 84–86
festival, distinct from feasting, 89
forbearance, distinct from fasting, 85
Foster, Richard, xi, 184n6
frugality, 48–49, 81

garrulity, 116. *See also* talkativeness
gluttony, 18, 78–80
gormandize. *See* gluttony
Grantchester (TV series), 99
Gregory the Great, xi, 88–89, 186n4 (chap. 4)

hoarding, 43, 44, 82, 185n5
Holy Spirit, 24, 35, 184n6 (chap. 1)
    conviction of, xiv, 16, 26, 37, 71, 75
    empowering of, 144
    guidance of, xii, xv, 16, 24, 52, 55, 93, 127
    life in, xi, xiv, 24–25, 31, 32, 35
    prompting of, 37, 75, 111, 158, 164
    work in creating, 23, 24, 26
    work of renewal, xiv, 16, 27, 106, 122–23
horizontal dimension of spiritual practices, xii, 13–14, 36, 50, 69, 87, 105, 122, 157, 167, 176
    definition, 9–14
Hughes, Langston, 80–81, 186n2
Hurricane Sandy, 50

image of God, xiv, xv, 25, 35
    and commandments, 26
    and communion, 111, 187n3
    and discipleship, 23
    neighbor as, 71, 110
individualism, 9, 12, 36, 56, 91, 122, 157, 167, 187n3 (chap. 5)
instrumentalism, 9, 123
intellectualism, 9, 12, 13, 36
intrusion, 97, 110
isolation, 108

Jesus
    and eating, 82, 89, 91
    and everyday life, xiv, 25, 28–29
    as image-bearer, 23
    as Judge, 23
    as King, 23, 158, 171
    as leader, xiii, xv, 20, 26
    and life in the Spirit, 24–25
    and living love, 30–32, 176, 177
    and offense, 5
    and owning, 44, 46, 52–53
    as Priest, 23
    as Prophet, 23
    as Redeemer, 23
    and resting, 152, 153, 155
    as Savior, 23, 169
    as second Adam, 23
    and socializing, 98, 100, 102, 104–6, 108
    as Son, 23
    spiritual disciplines, practicing, 15, 33, 35
    and talking, 117, 119, 126
    as teacher, xi, xiv, 22, 24, 26
    and thinking, 62, 64–65
    the way of, 14, 27, 29–30, 80, 173
    and working, 133, 134–36, 137, 138, 139
Judge, The (film), 97

Kant, Immanuel, 99
Kierkegaard, Søren, vii, xi, xvi, 2, 180, 183n5, 184n5, 185n8, 190

lavishness, 41, 43, 44, 45, 46, 49, 51, 52, 83, 178
laziness, 18, 103, 104, 132, 150–52, 153, 155, 160, 178
Little Miss Chatterbox (Hargreaves), 113–14, 116
liturgy, 171–74, 186n8, 188n1, 190
loquaciousness, 99, 116, 117, 118
love
    as common good, 176
    demonstrated by living for others, 14, 23, 29–32, 177–78, 185n8
    through eating, 80, 82, 91, 92
    through everyday activities, 28, 34, 35, 37, 171
    of Jesus, 33
    of neighbor, xi, xv
    through owning, 44, 46, 52–53, 55
    through resting, 152, 154, 162, 163
    of self, 15, 20
    through socializing, 98, 100, 104, 110
    through talking, 119, 123–24, 125–26
    through thinking, 63, 65, 71–74
    through working, 133, 135, 140, 141, 143–44
Luther (TV series), 27
luxury, 43

malice, 63, 123, 185n2
malignity, 33, 117, 118, 119, 124, 178

miserliness, 80–83, 88, 92,
   186n1 (chap. 4)
monopolization, 79–80,
   88, 178
Mouw, Richard, xi, 179,
   190
mundane activities, xv,
   16, 33, 36, 153, 171

negative emotions, 3, 4
negligence
   with coworkers, 132
   with work, 131, 132, 151

otherworking, 152–54, 160
owning, three aspects
   of, 45

parachurch organiza-
   tions, 55
Parks and Recreation (TV
   series), 67
Paul (apostle), 24, 70, 122,
   126, 137, 189
phone, xii, 111, 127, 154,
   164
Plato, 40, 65, 185nn3–4
politics, xiii, xv, 28, 29, 31,
   106, 125, 133, 169
   of spiritual disciplines,
   35, 170
"portable shops," 173
positive emotions, 3–4, 9
possessions, 41, 45–46,
   49–55
public, definition of,
   167–71
public affairs, Christian
   philosophy of, xii, xv
punishment. *See* discipline

recreation, distinct from
   rest, 156–57

renunciation, distinct
   from fasting, 48
rest, 147–65
Rousseau, Jean-Jacques,
   175, 188n2

sacrificial living, 24,
   31–32
Schilder, Klaas, 20, 184n4
Se7en (film), 79
seclusion, distinct from
   solitude, 102, 103
self-absorption, 61–63
Seneca, Lucius Annaeus,
   164, 187n2 (chap. 8)
sin, 24, 28, 29, 52, 123, 140
sleep, distinct from rest,
   155–56
Socrates, 40, 42–43
solitude, 102–4
   Thoreau on, 107–8
spirit and body, 23
spiritual disciplines
   defined, 26–27
   horizontal dimension,
   xii, 9–14, 36, 50, 69, 87,
   105, 122, 157, 167, 176
   Jesus as practicing, 15,
   33, 35
   politics of, 35, 170
spiritual euphoria, 7, 8
spiritual formation, 24–25
spiritual growth, 12–13
spiritual high, 7, 8, 14
squandering, 45, 46, 51,
   52–53, 178
stewardship, 23, 52, 53, 71,
   83, 91, 100, 123, 143
stimulation, 3, 4, 5, 8, 9, 14

talkativeness, 115–17, 119
   examples from popular
   culture, 116

"Target Lady" (*Saturday
   Night Live* skit), 115–16
temperance, distinct from
   fasting, 85
Thomas Aquinas, 51–52,
   185n7
Thoreau, Henry David,
   107–9, 187n2 (chap. 5)
"Three I's" of Christian
   practice, 9
time-out, 100–101

vacation
   distinct from rest, 148,
   154
   distinct from solitude,
   102–3
verbosity, 116
via vitae (way of life), 173
vice, 28, 117, 119, 189
   definition of, 17–18
visio vitae (vision for life),
   172

Willard, Dallas, xi, 190
Wirzba, Norman, 92, 142,
   185n9, 186n6 (chap. 4),
   187n4 (chap. 5), 190
worship
   and acts of love, 170, 172
   and all of life, 16, 178
   corporate, 3, 157, 158,
   172, 174
   formative aspect of, 190
   and positive emotions,
   4, 5
   Sabbath, 159–60, 162,
   163, 164
   as vehicle for wicked-
   ness, 12
   and work, 188n1

Zootopia (film), 150